THE
MARSHALL
PLAN
WORKBOOK

Writing Your Novel From Start to Finish

Evan Marshall

WRITER'S DIGEST BOOKS
CINCINNATI, OHIO
www.writersdigest.com

To my parents

Acknowledgments

I would like to thank my family, who patiently and lovingly allowed me to spend many a night at the computer as I worked on this book.

Special thanks also to Jack Heffron and Meg Leder at Writer's Digest Books, and to my agent, Maureen Walters, for their expert guidance.

The Marshall Plan Workbook, Writing Your Novel From Start to Finish.
Copyright © 2001 by Evan Marshall. Manufactured in the United States of America. All rights reserved. No part of this book may be reproduced in any form or by any electronic or mechanical means including information storage and retrieval systems without permission in writing from the publisher, except by a reviewer, who may quote brief passages in a review. Published by Writer's Digest Books, an imprint of F&W Publications, Inc., 1507 Dana Avenue, Cincinnati, Ohio 45207. (800) 289-0963. First edition.

Visit our Web site at www.writersdigest.com for information on more resources for writers.

To receive a free weekly e-mail newsletter delivering tips and updates about writing and about Writer's Digest products, send an e-mail with the message "Subscribe Newsletter" to newsletter-request@writersdigest.com or register directly at our Web site at www.writersdigest.com.

05   04   03   02   01   5   4   3   2

Library of Congress Cataloging-in-Publication Data

Marshall, Evan
    The marshall plan workbook / by Evan Marshall.—1st ed.
       p.   cm.
    Includes index.
    ISBN 1-58297-059-9 (alk. paper)
       1. Fiction—authorship. 2. Fiction—technique. I. Title.

PN3365.M285   2001
808.3—dc21   00-051323
                                                                   CIP

Edited by Jack Heffron and Meg Leder
Designed by Sandy Conopeotis Kent
Production coordinated by Mark Griffin

Other Books by Evan Marshall

- *Eye Language*
- *Hanging Hannah*
- *The Marshall Plan for Novel Writing*
  (published in Great Britain as *Novel Writing*)
- *Missing Marlene*
- *Stabbing Stephanie*

About the Author

Evan Marshall is the president of The Evan Marshall Agency, a leading literary agency that specializes in representing fiction writers. A former book editor and packager, he has contributed articles on writing and publishing to *Writer's Digest* and other magazines. He is the international best-selling author of *Eye Language, The Marshall Plan for Novel Writing* and the Jane Stuart and Winky series of mystery novels. He lives in Pine Brook, New Jersey.

Contents

About This Book

In my book *The Marshall Plan for Novel Writing*, I introduced a step-by-step novel-writing system that showed writers how to conceive a story idea, plot a novel using templates called section sheets, write their novel and market it.

The outpouring of responses my book has elicited from both beginning and veteran novelists has been overwhelming and extremely gratifying. These writers enjoy using the book's practical, hands-on approach, a refreshing change from abstract, theoretical novel-writing guides. Writers groups follow the Marshall Plan to write their novels. Some writers use the Plan to write short stories and screenplays.

Yet many readers have asked for something more—a book that shows how to use my system in even greater detail, that focuses on novel structure, in an interactive, workbook form.

That's what *The Marshall Plan Workbook* is: a refinement and enhancement of, as well as a complement to, *The Marshall Plan for Novel Writing*. In this book you'll find the Marshall Plan Blueprint, a revolutionary device engineered to guide you through a customized sequence of section sheets for you to complete in planning your novel. A Writing Coach feature on each page of the Blueprint helps you complete the sheets by offering pointers and instructions.

I've worked to make the Blueprint, with its preprogrammed, flowchart-based format, fun and easy to follow. Much calculating has been done for you behind the scenes, so that the Blueprint takes care of technical aspects and frees you to concentrate on more creative aspects of novel writing such as characterization and ingenuity of story idea. Just follow your "track" through this turnkey system—and leave the driving to the Blueprint!

But don't let this book's programmed format inhibit you. The Blueprint is a device to aid you in building your novel. If in places your creative instincts tell you to deviate from the Blueprint's structure, by all means do so. Throughout this book you'll also find many "rules" of novel writing. These, too, should be adapted to your needs. As in any other creative endeavor, these rules are sometimes meant to be judiciously broken. Be aware of them as general guidelines, but if you find you have good reason to ignore them, here too you should follow your instincts. Likewise, you'll undoubtedly think of examples of novels that break my rules or refute my advice—further proof that when all is said and done, a good story will win over agents, editors and readers every time.

I hope you find your journey through this workbook both enjoyable and productive.

A Word About *He* and *She*

Throughout this book I have alternated the use of *he* and *she*. I have abandoned, like so many authors, the arbitrary convention of using *he* exclusively. This convention of male exclusivity has lost its validity. I was tempted, when referring to readers, to refer solely to *she*, since the majority of readers are women; however, that would not have been fair either.

PART I

The Writing Life

CHAPTER 1

The Novelist's Mind-set

Achieving success as a novelist doesn't start with your talent and creativity or with your storytelling ability. It starts with how you *think* about being a novelist.

Defining Success

Some of the happiest and most fulfilled writers I know have reached what many would consider only a modest level of success—*success* being the operative word. Early in their careers, these writers defined (consciously or unconsciously) what success would mean for them. What would it take for them to feel they had achieved what they'd set out to achieve? They established these criteria realistically and according to their own definitions of writing success, not according to the image of "best-selling author" that many "civilians" hold but which few writers actually achieve. When they attained this success as they had defined it, they were fulfilled; they had "done it"; they were happy and at peace.

Sad to say, in my years as an editor and agent, I have known a large number of novelists who *have* achieved the public's stereotypical view of writing success but who are not at peace, not happy or creatively fulfilled by what they have accomplished. In fact, they are anything but. They are perpetually unhappy, driven by a desire to be richer, more famous, to sell more and more books, to make their publishers love them more. They are eaten up by envy of other writers' successes—the best-seller lists they've appeared on, the attention their publishers give them and so on. If you asked these unhappy writers what they're aiming for, what it would take to make them happy, they would have no answer because they don't really know; they've never stopped to figure out what success really means to *them*.

In today's world, it's difficult to have the self-confidence, self-esteem and self-possession to define for ourselves what constitutes success, what will make us feel satisfied and serene. We're bombarded by stories in the media about the megadeals that people just like us are getting. We read best-selling books that appear to be no better than the ones we're writing. We're afraid of the embarrassment we'll feel in the presence of our friends and relatives if we don't reach that canned image of the best-selling author.

But sitting down and digging deep into your own special desires, the forces that made you want to be a novelist in the first place, is the only way to ensure real success. What specific aspects of being a novelist are truly meaningful to you?

Sitting down and deciding that success for you as a novelist means being a number one *New York Times* best-seller is not what I'm talking about. You probably won't achieve this goal, because precious few do. I'm not trying to rain on your parade; I'm simply being realistic. Being realistic is the first key to setting your personal writing career goals. The writer who sets unrealistic goals and never achieves them dooms herself to a career full of frustration.

Start, then, with what's realistic.

Market Realities

Later in this book, we'll talk about deciding on the kind of novel you're best suited to write. Accept for the moment that there is one particular kind of novel you should be writing; for our purposes now, I'll simplify the issue by telling you that the kind of novel you should write is the kind of novel you most love to read.

You must honestly assess, to the best of your ability, the market potential for this kind of novel. We'll talk about goal setting in a moment. For now let's say, for example, that your main criterion for achieving personal success as a novelist is to hold your own hardcover novel in your hands. Yet your chosen genre of novel, the kind you always prefer to read, is the Regency romance. Being a Regency reader, you know that they are rarely, if ever, published in hardcover, unless you include the books of Georgette Heyer, or large-print or book club editions. Well, you're not Georgette Heyer, and although large-print and book club editions are indeed books, your novel being selected for either of these formats is by no means guaranteed. Your main goal for reaching personal success as a novelist is, therefore, unrealistic and likely to lead to frustration.

Let's take another example. The perfect novel for you to write is a young-adult novel—young-adult fantasy, to be precise. You want one of your YA fantasies to appear on a best-seller list—*The New York Times, USA Today, Publishers Weekly* . . . you're not fussy. But you're not being realistic. J.K. Rowling's Harry Potter books have done all of the above, but let's be honest: Few have before and few others will. To set this goal for yourself is to invite failure.

Another way in which you must be realistic in terms of setting goals within the context of the current market is with respect to money. People who know me or who have read my articles or *The Marshall Plan for Novel Writing* know I don't believe in writing just for money. Or to put it another way, I think it's foolhardy to write just for money. There's nothing wrong with wanting to be paid for producing something that makes money for others (publishers and booksellers) and entertains and gives people (readers) pleasure. But when you expect your writing to serve as the sole support for you, or you and your family, you're not only being unrealistic, you're also placing unfair pressure on yourself—pressure that, ironically, is likely to adversely affect your writing!

Any of us can name writers with healthy six-figure incomes who have no need to undertake any additional work to support themselves. And as an agent I can tell you that many writers who are patient eventually work their way up to advances and royalties large enough to live on.

But to expect this kind of monetary reward from your novels one, two or even five books into your career can be a big mistake. What you earn depends on a number of factors; the kind of book you're writing and how well your books sell are the two primary ones. The reality is that the majority of beginning novelists receive advances under ten thousand dollars—often *considerably* under—and in many cases these advances increase only slightly with each book. If you produce a novel a year, or even in slightly less time, you're nowhere near earning a living solely from your writing. Yes, there are romance writers who write four novels a year, receiving not only advances on these books but also royalties on past books. Collectively these payments constitute a respectable living for these writers. But the book market is erratic enough that even these writers are riding for a fall if they count on earning this same income, or a larger one, year after year. Publishers go out of business or merge with other publishers. They drop authors. They drop authors' advances. Authors slow down; life intrudes at the most unexpected times. To view writing as a job with a steady paycheck is a mistake that usually ends in bitter disillusionment.

Don't get me wrong. I'm not for a second saying you won't achieve great successes. You may. But in setting writing career goals, we must consider the odds: How likely is it, *realistically*, that we will reach these goals and thereby find the peace and creative fulfillment we seek?

To be truly reachable, goals must be set in the context of the current market.

Life Realities

Life has a habit of intruding on our creative endeavors. A novelist must set goals that are attainable within the limits of her or his lifestyle. This may sound obvious, but all too often writers fail to take the realities of their lives into consideration when deciding what to aim for in their careers.

For instance, a romance writer I knew decided early in her career that she would do whatever it took to get herself on *The New York Times* best-seller list—and I mean *whatever*. When she wasn't writing, she was moving rapidly around the country on a self-scheduled tour that included bookstore signings and speeches to various writers groups. Even during this tour, when she wasn't "on," she would run up to her hotel room and get some writing done on her notebook computer. During the few months of the year when she was at home, she would fly off at a second's notice to sign copies of her books in some wholesaler's warehouse—thousands of books at a time, until she needed medical attention for carpal tunnel syndrome.

But she didn't stop there. She underwent a radical "makeover," transforming herself from an average-looking person to a glamorous icon of romance. She appeared at conferences in provocatively tight dresses and cavorted with male romance-cover models in an effort to create publicity.

Admirable, you might say. There was just one problem: She had a husband and several young children. Her children, left for months at a time in the care of their father and a nanny, soon began to suffer the effects of their mother's neglect. Her husband, as supportive as any spouse can be expected to be, resented her prolonged absences, not to mention her public flirtations, and told her so. Before long this writer's marriage was falling apart. The stress of being pulled, physically and emotionally, between her career and her personal life took its toll, to the point that she needed psychiatric attention.

What had gone wrong? This writer had failed to set goals within the context of her world's realities—children, a husband, responsibilities. If she had discussed her goals and plans with her husband and children ahead of time, explaining exactly what these goals and plans would entail, perhaps things would have gone differently. But from the sale of her first novel to her first appointment with the therapist, she had behaved as if she was alone in the world. She failed to take into account the demands already present in her life. I don't have to tell you that this mistake led to frustration, to say the least.

What are the realities of *your* life? Are you on your own, with no one to answer to, or do you have children and a spouse to whom you've made a commitment of time and energy? If you're on your own, in all likelihood you are your own sole support, which means it would be foolhardy to quit your day job, as the saying goes, before knowing for certain that your writing will support you. And if you can't quit that day job, your writing time is obviously more limited than it would be if you didn't have to work.

If there are others in your world who expect things from you, consider exactly what they expect. Make a list. When, realistically, will you be able to get your writing done? Will the people in your life accept what you must do for your writing career? Can you work out an understanding with them, so that nothing you may find yourself doing in the name of success comes as a surprise they may resent? Often it's the writer with a securely employed spouse or partner who has the luxury of devoting time to a writing career that may not bring in much income at the beginning. But if you're in such a situation, make sure you spell out exactly what your partner will be underwriting, or you may be inviting the kind of resentment the poor writer above experienced.

Setting realistic goals in the context of your life's realities, then, means taking time and money into consideration. Accept that there is only so much you can do. If you're rich and without ties, what you can do may be a lot. If you're like most people, you'll have to fit writing into a life of limitations and other responsibilities. Accepting these, and setting your career goals accordingly, is an important component of success for a writer.

Your Personal Goals

The most important factor to take into consideration as you set your goals is that we each have a different definition of success. For one writer, success may be earning $100,000 a year solely from his writing. For another, success may be simply being able to hold her book in her hand and say, "I did it."

To define *your* picture of writing success, think hard about what made you want to write in the first place. Did you:

- Want to be famous?
- Want to make a lot of money?
- Need the ego gratification of seeing your work in print?
- Have a desire to entertain or move people with your stories?
- Crave the creative fulfillment of writing, whether you got published or not?

If you're like most people, you had a combination of reasons for wanting to write. Take some time now to search deep inside yourself for the reasons you first wanted to write.

When I *first* dreamed of a writing career, what I wanted from it most was:

1. _____

2. _____

3. _____

4. _____

5. _____

6. _____

7. _____

8. _____

9. _____

10. _____

Are these still your prime motivators for wanting to write novels? Have your goals changed? If they have, ask yourself whether it's because your dreams have truly evolved or because you've been influenced by that stereotypical picture of writing success that is, in truth, a rarity. When you perform the next exercise, answer the question as if none of those outside influences existed. Answer it as if you had only yourself to please, without regard for what others might think of your goals.

Today, when I dream of a writing career, what I want from it most is:

1. _____

2. _____

3. _____

4. _____

5. _____

6. _____

7. _____

8. _____

9. _____

10. _____

A Practical Dream

Now it's time to synthesize all of these factors—market and life realities, and your own picture of success—into a set of goals for your writing career.

In setting these goals, ask yourself the following two questions:

1. Based on my knowledge of the market for the novels I want to write, what are realistic milestones to strive for? (Examples of possible answers: To get published and keep on getting published with a commercial publisher. To see my book on a certain best-seller list—regional, national, industry, etc. Simply to get my novel into printed book form, to be able to hold it in my hands, even if I decide to self-publish. To get good reviews. To touch and entertain readers.)

2. Are these goals achievable within the structure of my life?

Are they consistent with choices I've made and responsibilities I have with respect to family and finances?

In setting your writing career goals, create a picture in your mind of this practical, achievable dream. What would your life be like? Adjust it if you like. Then, when it's the way your want it, write it down in the space provided on page 12.

Here's one writer's picture:

My Personal Writing Career Dream

In my personal writing career dream, I see myself publishing category romances, the short, "sweet" type (for example, Harlequin or Silhouette Romances), at the rate of roughly one every ten months. I would like to do bookstore signings in my local area and participate in panel discussions and book-signing events sponsored by Romance Writers of America and *Romantic Times* magazine. I want the pleasure of being able to show my family that I have writing talent and am "special" in this way, and I also want the satisfaction of having my readers sometimes write to me or come up to me and tell me that my stories have touched them in some way.

The career dream picture of the writer in the example above is perhaps, by the standards of some "civilians," modest. It is also completely honest. This writer has clearly searched her soul to determine exactly what will constitute her personal success. Interestingly, she makes no mention of money.

One final point to keep in mind as you devise your career dream picture is that you should determine the *least* it would take for you to feel you've succeeded. This picture, within the context of your chosen market and of your life, should be eminently realistic. But it doesn't have to be your final picture; it's just your first one. Once you've turned your career dream picture into reality, you can create a new, loftier one. The picture you're devising now is *for now*.

Reread your career dream picture often. Cherish it as the touchstone of your work as a novelist.

My Personal Writing Career Dream

In my personal writing career dream, I see myself . . .

CHAPTER 2

Time and Place for the Novelist

Now that you've clarified your novelist's mind-set, you should create a "world" around you that is conducive to this mind-set and conducive to you reaching your goals. Your world as a novelist is not just a physical one, though this aspect is, of course, important. It also comprises how you schedule your writing life and how you work with time.

Where Will You Write?

One of novel writing's greatest appeals is that you can do it virtually anywhere. Few of us—when we're starting out, at least—have the kind of dream office that civilians imagine novelists have. Most people have an image of the novelist comfortably ensconced in a book-lined office or study, perhaps with an ergonomically designed desk that provides space for a computer, printer, manuscripts and research materials. Maybe there's a picture window with a view of woods or a mountain vista or a peaceful meadow—or the novelist's enormous free-form pool (most civilians also think novelists are rich).

A few novelists have workspaces like this, but most don't. In fact, most people would be shocked to learn where most novels really get written. Many novelists I represent started by lugging a manual typewriter to the kitchen table. Others set up a card table in the bedroom, the living room, the grown-up child's room or the basement. Other writers have never had a stationary writing place: They compose in longhand in notebooks or on pads of paper on buses, trains and subways; they write at their desk at work during lunch hour and wherever they happen to be when the children are finally in bed. Recently I read an article about a young man who had just sold his first novel—a novel written in the quiet moments during his job operating a freight elevator. (His work space definitely had its ups and downs!)

The common quality you'll find among these novelists is determination. It didn't really matter *where* they wrote; what mattered was that they were disciplined enough to devote time to their writing that most people would devote to any number of other activities. It was also important that they kept at it; they were consistent.

The "perfect" writing place is, in truth, a rarity. Most people who say they want to write use the lack of such an ideal space as an excuse not to write "yet." As you saw from the previous examples, the people who really wanted to write found a way—anywhere and anytime they could.

And so should you. Think hard about the structure of your daily life, and look for places you could get writing done—if not in large blocks of uninterrupted time, then in lots of small ones. If you're fortunate enough to have a space in your home that you can devote to your writing, make it clear to others in your home that this space is private. You should be able to stop work and leave everything as you want it, without worrying that your materials will be disturbed. If such a permanent spot is not possible, consider the other places your life takes you where you could write. Anyone, if he thinks hard enough, can come up with at least one place. Often the key is to decide to write in a place where you've traditionally done something else.

The writers who create novels on buses, trains and subways, for example, undoubtedly once used these places for other purposes—reading a book, magazine or newspaper, doing a crossword puzzle, looking out the window, napping, daydreaming, chatting (even playing cards) with other regulars. A parent who used to watch every moment of her child's gymnastics/ballet/dance class might instead sit quietly with a spiral notebook, looking up and smiling every so often. Sometimes polite assertiveness is necessary when people accustomed to receiving your undivided attention are suddenly abandoned. If you're shy about revealing it's a novel you're creating, tell a white lie. It's something you've got to get done for work or a letter you've been meaning to write. Be firm and smile. Most people will nod and smile back. Writing on your lunch hour at work can be awkward if you're tapping away on a computer in full public view or if your boss resents your writing in the office even on your own time. In this case, leave! Sit in the company cafeteria, on a bench outside, in a restaurant or coffee shop or in your car.

Have you mentally gone through your entire day, both during the work week and on weekends, and scouted out every possible place for writing? Once you've arrived at the *where*, you must consider the *when*.

When Will You Write?

Ideally, you'll set up a regular schedule. For example, you'll *always* work on your novel on the bus or on that bench near your company's parking lot. Absolute consistency is not, of course, always possible. People and events have a habit of popping up. For this reason, I never advise committing to writing every single day, nor do I agree with those who insist you're not a writer unless you do. Nonsense. Take the time when it's available. If polite assertiveness won't work in some situations or if emergencies arise, accept this state of affairs and know you'll grab this moment next time.

You've got to be assertive with yourself, too. Do your best to use those blocks of time when they're available. It may take self-discipline not to skip your writing session on a particularly beautiful day when you'd rather use that time on the bench to take a walk or simply look around and enjoy nature. Make a promise to yourself that, whenever possible, you'll take advantage of the pieces of writing time you've carved out for yourself throughout the day.

Consider creating more of these pieces of writing time by *converting time*. If you're like most people, watching television consumes many of the hours in your week. Reassign some or all of your television time to writing. I almost never watch television. If I did, my books wouldn't get written. My books are more important to me by far. People ask me how I'm able to run my literary agency and still write my books and devote time to my family and friends. Dropping television is one of the ways.

What other of your activities consume time you could convert to writing time? Don't become a hermit or drop your social and leisure activities altogether, but consider honestly the ways you might devote more of your life to writing.

Even sleeping time should be scrutinized. Be careful not to lengthen your days to the extent that you're not getting enough sleep—a serious problem among Americans today—but ask yourself whether you may be getting more sleep than you need. The older we get, the less sleep we require. Are you going to bed and arising at certain times simply out of old habit rather than out of necessity? Do you really have to sleep late on Saturday and Sunday? Of course not. You may *want* to, but do you need to? What's more important to you, achieving your writing career goals or sleeping in?

Once, at a writers conference, I met a successful and prolific young writer of westerns who told me the secret to his success was having given up watching television and going to the movies. He found himself with hours and hours of time to be actively creative instead of passively entertained. He still made sure he spent time with his wife and young children.

Follow this writer's example and select those nonwriting activities that truly matter to you. Drop the rest. Most important to me is devoting time out of the office to being with my family, socializing with close friends, exercising and reading. When I'm not doing any of these things, chances are I'm writing. The key is to strike a balance borne of a hard-nosed assessment of what matters most to you. Since you're reading this book, I assume that being a successful novelist is high on your list of the things that matter.

Your Special Writing World

I use the word *special* because your writing world is exactly that—a world special to you, crafted from the places and times in your daily life that are conducive to writing. To make this world more real to you, use the Writing Time and Place Chart on page 18. You'll find an example of one novelist's Writing Time and Place Chart on page 17.

Obviously, you will not always be able to adhere to exactly the same schedule day after day, week after week. Emergencies arise. But if, for example, you are accustomed to devoting two hours every Sunday afternoon to writing, and that's entered on your Writing Time and Place Chart, you're more likely to decline an invitation to a movie or some other distraction in favor of keeping this appointment you've made with yourself.

Now that you've got a clear picture of your special writing world—the times and places you can devote to writing your novel—there's nothing stopping you from getting started on building your story, the subject of Part II.

Writing Time and Place Chart		
WEEKDAYS	**WHEN**	**WHERE**
	5:30–6:00 A.M. (before Al and kids get up)	kitchen table
	7:20–8:00 A.M.	train to Boston
	12:00–1:00 P.M. (except every other Friday—department lunch)	Bagel Stop
	5:45–6:25 P.M.	train home
	9:30–10:30 P.M.	bedroom
Total Writing Time in Day	3 hours 50 minutes	
Total Writing Time Monday–Friday	Approx. 19 hours	
WEEKENDS—Saturday	**WHEN**	**WHERE**
	10:00–11:30 A.M.	parking lot during Jeffrey's soccer practice
	3:00–4:00 P.M.	museum coffee shop during Christa's art lesson
Sunday	**WHEN**	**WHERE**
	2:00–4:00 P.M.	living room
	9:30–10:30 P.M.	bedroom
Total Writing Time in Weekend	5½ hours	
TOTAL WRITING TIME IN WEEK	24½ hours	

Writing Time and Place Chart		
WEEKDAYS	**WHEN**	**WHERE**
Total Writing Time in Day		
Total Writing Time Monday–Friday		
WEEKENDS—Saturday	**WHEN**	**WHERE**
Sunday	**WHEN**	**WHERE**
Total Writing Time in Weekend		
TOTAL WRITING TIME IN WEEK		

PART II

Story Preliminaries

CHAPTER 3

The Market-Savvy Novelist

In Part I we discussed setting writing career goals and fitting writing into your life in order to achieve success as a novelist. But that's only half of the success equation. The other half is attaining a true understanding of the market you're creating for—understanding the business of publishing novels. For without also gaining this understanding—without being willing to accept the cold truths of this industry you've decided to break into—you're just as doomed to failure and frustration.

Book Business

Writing novels is an art; few will argue this point. It's an art some writers master with exquisite skill and subtlety. Consider two other art forms: painting and screenwriting. Some practitioners of these art forms also achieve outstanding mastery. But these three art forms—novel writing, painting and screenwriting—differ from one another in an important way: control, the artist's ability to determine all aspects of how his creation is presented to the world.

At one end of the control spectrum is painting. The painter creates a work, and only when the painter decides it's finished does it leave the studio. From there it probably goes to a gallery, where it's displayed under conditions (lighting, location, etc.) about which the artist may be consulted. When an individual purchases the painting, the painter relinquishes all control; it is now up to the buyer to determine how and where the painting will be displayed and enjoyed.

At the other end of the control spectrum is screenwriting. By necessity, making a film requires a large number of individuals who contribute their various talents to the creation of the film—from the actors to the art director, from the director to the camera operators, with count-less people in between. As a result, a film rarely if ever exactly resem-bles the original artistic vision of the screenwriter while writing the screenplay.

On the control spectrum, novel writing is somewhere in the middle. Like the painter, the novelist retains her creation until she feels it's ready and complete. But a novel, unlike a painting, then becomes sub-ject to a number of processes that are beyond the novelist's control. Sometimes, to one degree or another, the novelist is invited to become involved in some of these processes, but more often this is not the case. The publisher, theoretically, is expert in the packaging and selling of novels; it expects the author to respect this expertise and let the pub-lisher do what it does best, without interference. Novelists who do not accept this reality, this necessary relinquishment of control of their creative work, meet with frustration and a sense of impotence. Worse, if they make too much of a nuisance of themselves, they may find themselves without a publisher.

I know what you're thinking. "But it's my book; my name will go on it. I have a right to a say in how it's presented to the world." To an extent, this is true. For example, a responsible publisher will work to arrive at a title for a novel that is satisfactory to both the publisher and the author, and will not arbitrarily decide on a title without consulting the author first. A responsible publisher will also consult the author on matters of editing and copyediting, and won't make changes to a manuscript without the author's approval. A responsible publisher will at least take into consideration concerns or objections an author may have about his novel's jacket or cover.

But that's usually about as far as it goes. The shrewd novelist will adopt as her mantra the first line of the "Serenity Prayer" of Alcoholics Anonymous: "God, grant me the serenity to accept the things I cannot change. . . ." There's that word again: *serenity*. I believe it's the condi-tion most crucial to a novelist's personal and professional success.

Be willing to let go, then, of those aspects of publishing a novel that are rightfully within the publisher's purview. Accept that:

• Your editor will almost always ask you to revise your novel after it's under contract. Resist the knee-jerk "I won't do it" response. Try to put your work at an objective arm's length and consider the changes you've been asked to make. Chances are good they'll be to your novel's benefit. But if you don't like a suggestion—if you really don't believe in your heart of hearts that it's a good idea—ask your editor why she wants the change. Then, if you agree with her reasoning, come up with your own way to address her concern.

• You will be shown your manuscript after it has been edited and/or after it has been copyedited, for your approval. You will not initially like every change that's been made to your prose. Try to be objective: Has the editing improved your work? Ideally, in nearly all cases the answer to this question will be "yes." When it's not, follow the previous procedure: Find out why the change was made (a point was repetitive/awkward/unclear, for example), and devise a correction that works for *you*.

• Your novel's jacket or cover proof may bear no resemblance to what you envisioned for your book (if you envisioned anything at all), or you may feel it's just all wrong. Know that in matters of jacket or cover art, typeface, placement of type (most notably your name and the novel's title), cover or jacket copy, colors and a myriad of other aspects, your publisher has more experience than you do about what sells (and doesn't sell) books. Ideally everything on your jacket or cover was done for a good reason. If you are truly convinced that your cover or jacket is all wrong, or if you have a suggestion for a change you firmly believe is important—and remembering that changes cost the publisher money that reduces the bottom line (more on this below) and thus your profitability—then call your agent if you have one, or if you don't, make the call yourself. But tread softly and tactfully, and be prepared for the possibility that you might lose.

• Your novel, at least when you are starting out in your career, may receive little or no publicity or promotion. Know and accept that the lion's share of a publisher's publicity and promotion budget goes to the books "at the top of the list"—the brand names, the best-sellers. Know also that it is helpful for you to conduct your own publicity and promotion to the best of your ability and within your means; in fact, publishers today *expect* you to.

• When all is said and done, the bottom line is the bottom line: in other words, how well your books sell. Your novels may receive critical acclaim, but if they are not commercial successes, after a while your publisher may drop you. Moreover, know that especially in situations such as this, your editor, publicist and anyone else on your publisher's staff are your business associates first, *then* perhaps your friends. If business realities dictate that they drop you as an author or perpetrate some other acts detrimental to your career (publish you less frequently, decrease your advances, lower your position on the list), these people will do so because that is the job they're paid by the publisher to do. This is not to say that you cannot be friends with people on your publisher's staff. Just that you're well advised to remember that in these cases, business and friendship have nothing to do with each other.

Rules of the Game

Serenity, though, isn't the only result of understanding and accepting how publishing novels works. Before serenity will come book contracts. If you don't conform to certain conventions with respect to how you create your novels and conduct yourself as a businessperson, you may never get the book contracts that lead to serenity.

What are these conventions? Specific genres of novels have conventions of their own, which we'll discuss in the next chapter, but following is a list of the conventions that apply to all novels. You'll find that each of them relates in some way to conforming to reader expectations. The reader is, after all, your ultimate customer—and the customer is always right!

Fit a Specific Genre

It must be instantly clear to any and all who read your novel exactly what kind of novel it is. What is its genre? In the following chapter you'll find a list of genres. It's important that your story fit into one of them, which means you must have a specific genre in mind when you set out to create your book. Mixing genres that aren't usually mixed is a creative adventure I discourage beginning writers from undertaking; there are already enough established "cross-genre" mutations (for instance, futuristic romance). You shouldn't need to try breeding a hybrid of your own.

You must be able to visit any large bookstore and find the section where your novel will be shelved after it has been published. (To make the dream even more real, find the spot exactly where your book will be placed alphabetically and insert your finger into this space, creating a book-width opening—an opening for *your* novel. Before my first novel was published, I enjoyed performing this exercise and at the same time whispering, "Someday, fellas, someday," to the books on either side of my finger. Good thing no one was standing nearby, or my sanity might have been seriously questioned. Anyway, the day finally arrived when I walked into that store and there, in the space where I'd always inserted my finger, saving a place for my imaginary book, was my book itself. It was a wonderful feeling.)

Why must your book fall so cleanly into a specific genre? One reason has just been stated—so that bookstores will know where to put you. Why is that important? So readers who like to read in your genre will find you! Because booksellers think in these category-specific terms, so do publishers, and so therefore do the agents who sell to these publishers, and so therefore do writers in order to attract one of these agents. It's just good old practical common sense.

Conform to Mechanical Conventions

No, mechanical conventions aren't robot reunions. They're the physical aspects of novels that readers have come to expect and prefer.

Length

One of these aspects is your novel's length. For every genre there is a correct "word length," to use the common industry expression. Make it your business to learn the correct word length for the type of book you're writing. Some publishers of "lines" of books—for example, Silhouette, Harlequin, Kensington and Leisure—offer a prepared set of guidelines, or a "tip sheet," to anyone who sends a request with a self-addressed stamped envelope. These tip sheets invariably state the correct word length or range of word length for the line of books it's discussing.

If the kind of novel you're writing isn't a "line" book and therefore has no tip sheet, gather a half dozen published books as close as possible in genre and feel to the one you're contemplating. Calculate the word length of each book and average them. To calculate the word length of a published book, follow my tried-and-true formula:

Number of Pages in Book $\times$ Number of Lines
on a Full Page $\times$ 9 = Word Length

Once you have a target word length, you can figure out how many manuscript pages that number translates into by dividing the word length by 250, the average number of words on a typical double-spaced manuscript page (twenty-five lines per page; 1¼″ left and right margins). A 100,000-word novel, then, is 400 pages; a 75,000-word novel, 300 pages; a 55,000-word novel, 220 pages; and so on. You'll need these numbers later, so record them here:

Target word length: _____ words.

Number of manuscript pages: _____.

Manuscript Preparation

A properly prepared manuscript not only signifies that you're a professional, but it also facilitates the jobs of your agent, editor and production person. Your agent and editor will be able to read your manuscript easily, concentrating on your story rather than on how it's presented. Your editor will be able to edit your manuscript between the lines if it's double-spaced and jot queries to you if the margins are wide enough. Your publisher's production person will be able to perform a "castoff" (a calculation of the number of characters in your manuscript) if your pages are uniform in terms of line length and number of lines.

In my experience, professional writers make themselves known not so much by what they do as by what they *don't* do. It's the amateurs, for instance, who take full advantage of their word-processing programs' desktop publishing capabilities by making their manuscripts look like actual printed books, complete with justified (even) left and right margins, fancy and/or oversize display type for titles and chapter numbers, and intricate symbols and decorations to indicate space breaks.

In actuality, your manuscript should be blessedly simple. Justify only your left-hand margin; keep the right-hand margin uneven, or "ragged." Don't hyphenate words at the end of lines.

Purists prefer text in the good old Courier font reminiscent of the IBM Selectric, rather than proportional fonts such as Times Roman. This is because Courier allots the same amount of space to every character, which makes performing a castoff easier. Titles should also be in Courier font, upper and lowercase. Indicate that a word should be italicized by underlining it; do not use actual italics. Never use boldface.

Use plain white paper and print on one side only. Double-space everything in your manuscript (except a few lines on your title page, which I'll address presently). At the top of every page except the title page (about half an inch from the edge), type in the upper left-hand corner a "slug line" consisting of your name and, in all capital letters, the title of your novel. At the right-hand margin, on the same line, type the page number, without dashes, periods or the word "Page," like this:

Anderson/BRED IN THE BONE	5

wouldn't have given it a second thought if she hadn't looked at him like that. "Do you see that tree just over there?" she asked, pointing with

Start the numbering on the page following the title page, and continue consecutively throughout the manuscript. Do not number chapters separately. Set your left and right margins at 1¼″ and adjust your top and bottom margins until your word processor places twenty-five lines on each page. To start a new chapter, type just the number of the chapter, spelled out, in the center of the page, halfway down. Double-space twice and begin the text. Indent all paragraphs half an inch. Do not leave extra space between paragraphs.

Make sure your word processor's "widow and orphan control" is turned off. (A widow is the last line of a paragraph typed by itself at the top of a page; an orphan is the first line of a paragraph typed by itself at the bottom of a page.) These are avoided in printed books but preferable in manuscripts for uniform page length. This is a manuscript, not a book; it should look like a manuscript.

To create a title page for your manuscript, type single-spaced (the only place this is allowed) in the upper left-hand corner of the page your name, address, telephone and fax numbers and your e-mail address if you have one. If you have an agent, type your name in care of your agent's name, address, phone, fax, etc. In the upper right-hand corner of the page, type the manuscript's word length, rounded to the nearest 5,000 words. Halfway down the page, center your novel's title in all capital letters. Double-space and center "A Novel by." Double-space and center your name. If you're using a pseudonym, type that instead of your real name.

Present your manuscript pages loose, not bound or clipped in any way, in a manuscript, typing paper or printer paper box. That's about it. No colored paper, binders, clips, yarn, ribbons, twine, crumpled newspaper or packing peanuts. No perfumed pages. No colored type other than black. No photo of yourself tucked beneath the title page. I could go on and on. Why? Because as an editor and agent, I've seen all of the above and then some. All of these extraneous preparations and prettifications mark the submitter as an amateur and send negative psychological signals to the person opening your manuscript. Why start out with any strikes against you, especially when the professional way is the simplest and easiest way of all?

Understand That Fast Is As Important As Good

One area of novel writing in which art and commercialism often clash involves speed. Art, many novelists say, cannot be rushed; yet once a writer makes a sale, his publisher will in all likelihood expect him to deliver novels at the rate of approximately one a year. It's difficult to build a writer's career and boost sales if books are published much farther than a year apart. Even a year is longer than many publishers prefer; some of the romance writers I represent deliver from two to four top-quality manuscripts a year, and their publishers release these books at the same rate.

But in most cases publishers acknowledge that writers usually need about a year to conceive and write a novel, and a writer who delivers at this rate is in good shape. Readers come to expect a book from their favorite authors about once a year. These authors become a "habit" for these readers. The authors' names appear on the market frequently enough to register on the public's consciousness, and sales build.

To expect success as a novelist, then, you must accept that although novel writing is an art of the highest order, the demands of commercialism must be met. You must not only be good but also fast. This becomes easier over time. You will learn that although the writing and revision processes can go on literally forever as you make your novel better and better, it's more important to know when to stop, to recognize that your novel needs to be finished more than it needs to be perfect, in the interest of time.

If you're like most writers, you will make your first sale on the basis of a complete manuscript. Subsequently, however, you will be able to sell novels on the strength of a proposal (a synopsis and the first few, usually three, chapters), or on nothing at all. You, your agent and your publisher will arrive at delivery dates—deadlines by which your manuscripts must be submitted to the publisher. You'll want to keep in mind the importance of frequent publication when you set these delivery dates. Then, just as important, you'll want to work hard to honor them.

Deliver the Goods

Of course you'll deliver, and of course it will be good, you're thinking; we've just talked about that. But now I'm talking about something else. I'm talking about writing a novel that "delivers."

Delivers what? A moving, compelling, entertaining story that is fresh within readers' genre expectations. Novels are entertainment in a world filled with more forms of entertainment than we've ever known. Readers want to have fun with your novel, to escape into the world you've created for them. And they want to put down your book with a feeling of satisfaction.

How can you achieve these qualities in your novel? We'll go into specifics shortly, but in general the key is to keep characters' emotions at the forefront; write about issues, whether large or small, that people care about; tell your story in an interesting manner; pay attention to your story's pacing; and wind up your novel on a satisfying note. You will be writing the kind of novel you most like to read, but you will also be writing to please your readers. Never forget this. To ignore the requirements of an entertaining story in favor of indulging your own desires is to flirt with career failure.

In the next chapter we'll talk about another important aspect of being a market-savvy novelist: choosing the right story genre for you.

CHAPTER 4

Genres and How to Choose One

E arlier I touched on the subject of genres when I said you should write what you most love to read. There are several good reasons to do this:

1. You'll have a good idea of what kinds of stories have and haven't been done in this genre.

2. Your enjoyment of books in this genre will translate into a real passion for what you're writing. You'll be writing the kind of book you most want to read, thus producing a sincere project.

Later I advised you to make sure your book fits clearly into a specific genre, because the book business is "genre driven"; readers, booksellers, publishers, agents and therefore you as a novelist must think in these terms.

If you asked the average reader to name the various genres that exist in fiction, she would probably rattle off a handful: mystery, romance, horror, science fiction. For our purposes, these broad categories aren't specific enough. You may not be aware of it, but the novels you most love to read aren't just mysteries or romances or horror or science fiction. You may think you're reading romance, but you are actually reading *contemporary* or *historical* romance. And it doesn't end there. If you read contemporary romance, in all likelihood you enjoy a specific *kind* of contemporary romance best—for example, short "sweet," mainstream, or romantic comedy.

Why does it matter? Because when you know the exact subcategory of the novels you love to read and will write, you will have an even sharper fix on your market. This in turn will enable you to please readers and to target prospective literary agents and editors more intelligently. Following is a list of virtually all of the genres and subgenres of fiction you're likely to encounter. If you read *The Marshall Plan for Novel Writing*, you'll recall an earlier version of this list. To the one following I have added a number of new subgenres.

ACTION/ADVENTURE

Mercenary   War

Survivalist

CHRISTIAN

Biblical   Mystery

Contemporary   Mystery/Romance

Frontier Romance   Romance

Historical

FANTASY

Alternate History   Medieval

Contemporary   Military

Dark   Modern

Epic   Science

Gay   Sociological

High   Speculative Science

Humorous   Fiction/Fantasy

Lesbian   Traditional

Light   Urban

Magic Realism

GAY/LESBIAN

Coming-of-Age   Romance

Erotica   Science Fiction

Mystery   Suspense

Relationship

HISTORICAL

Biographical   Family Saga

Frontier

General

Generational Saga

Multicultural

Prehistoric

Saga

Western

HORROR

Contemporary

Crime

Dark

Erotica

Humorous

Light

Modern

Occult

Paranormal

Psychological

Technological

Traditional

Urban

MAINSTREAM

Biographical

Crime

Erotica

Feminist

Glitz and Glamour

Humor/Satire

Literary

Magic Realism

Military/War

New Age

Occult

Paranormal

Political

Sequel to/Completion of Classic

Speculative

Sports

Supernatural

Women's

MYSTERY

Amateur Detective

Biographical Historical

Comic Caper

Courtroom/Trial

Cozy

Crime

Dark

Espionage

Fact-Based Contemporary

Fact-Based Historical

Hard-Boiled Detective

Historical

Humorous

Literary

Malice Domestic

Police Procedural

Private Detective

Puzzle

Senior Sleuth

Surrealistic

ROMANCE

Americana	Multicultural Contemporary
Angel	Multicultural Historical
Edwardian	Nurse
Erotic	Pirate Historical
Fantasy	Regency
Futuristic	Regency Historical
Georgian	Reincarnation
Ghost	Romantic Comedy
Gothic	Romantic Suspense
Historical Adventure	Short Humorous Contemporary
Historical Romance	Short Sensual Contemporary
Inspirational Contemporary	Short Sweet Contemporary
Inspirational Historical	Time Travel
Long Sensual Contemporary	Vampire
Magic	Victorian
Mainstream Contemporary	Viking
Mature Contemporary	Western Historical
Medieval	

SCIENCE FICTION

Adventure	Humorous
Alternative	Military
Anthropological/Genetic	Mystery-Related
Apocalyptic	Offbeat
Avant-Pop	Postmodern
Cyberpunk	Psychological
Cybertek	Religious
Dark Fantasy	Sociological
Darkly Humorous	Space Opera
Erotica	Speculative
Experimental	Steampunk
Fantasy	Surreal/Mood
Feminist	Time Travel
Futuristic	Traditional
Hard	Urban Horror
Harsh Parody	Weird
Horrific	

SUSPENSE

Crime	Political Thriller
Domestic	Psychological
Erotic Thriller	Psychosexual Thriller
Espionage	Serial-Killer Thriller
Legal Thriller	Techno-Thriller
Medical Thriller	Thriller
Paranormal Thriller	Woman-in-Jeopardy

WESTERN

Adult	Military
Biographical	Traditional
Fact-Based	

YOUNG ADULT

Adventure	Humor
Biographical	Mystery
Coming-of-Age	Mystery Romance
Contemporary	Problem
Ethnic	Romance
Fantasy	Science Fiction
Historical	Suspense
Horror	Western

Think about the books you most enjoy reading. What subgenre do they fit into? You may already know. If not, do some research to find out. Read reviews (which often classify a book) or speak to knowledgeable booksellers and librarians.

Once you're able to state with confidence, "I love to read _____," set a program for yourself of continuing to read in this specific subgenre. This isn't to say you shouldn't read anything else; but you must keep reading in the particular area you'll be targeting with your writing in order to stay aware of what sorts of stories are being told and how the genre may be changing. The most successful novelists make it their business to keep up a reading program of this kind, and you should, too. You'll be market aware, and this market awareness will give you an edge over others, an edge that will increase your chances of getting published sooner and of *continuing* to get published.

CHAPTER 5

The Crisis—Where Your Story Begins

Every story, whether from real life or in a novel or film, starts with a crisis, an event that upsets the normal order of things for the subject of that story, the lead. The story itself is an account of how the lead overcomes a series of obstacles and ultimately achieves a goal that will restore her life to its normal, happy state.

Many of the novels submitted to my agency contain no crisis. The story just meanders aimlessly, recounting events in a person's or several people's lives, with no driving force behind these events or these characters' actions. The characters aren't doing the things they're doing for one, unifying reason. Very often I sense that these books are based on someone's actual life, most likely that of the writer. Many writers who create stories like this defend them by saying, "But those things really happened."

It doesn't matter. A novel is not merely an account of a portion of one or more persons' lives. A novel takes life and puts it into a form that qualifies as a story: person seeking goal that will solve a crisis. Drawing *ideas* for novels from real life is not only acceptable; it's most often the way novels are born. But slicing out a piece of a life and calling it a novel never works.

Before you can devise a crisis that will set your story in motion, you must define your lead. Why? Because whether or not an event *is* a crisis depends largely on who is experiencing that event.

Your novel, by the way, must have a lead character. A surprising number of manuscripts submitted to my agency have no clearly defined lead. Either the story is about a number of people, all of whom the writer has given equal importance in the story, or two or three characters stand out equally, so that the story seems to have several leads.

Neither approach works. A novel must be about one person's quest to attain a goal, and it must be clear that this person's actions are of primary importance in the story.

Begin, then, by creating a basic definition of your lead: gender and age.

Gender

Think about the novels you read in your target genre. Is the lead always or more often male or female? If your target genre is romance, for example, your lead should probably be female. If your target genre is western, your lead should probably be male. If you've noticed no predominance of male or female leads, you have a choice. You may choose one gender over another because you think you'll feel more comfortable writing about one over the other. Or you may already have in mind the seed of a story idea that lends itself better to either a male or female lead.

Age

You needn't decide on an exact age now. You must simply specify whether your lead is an adult or a teenager, a child or a senior citizen. If you're writing a novel for adults, your lead probably should be an adult. Generally speaking, grown-ups want to read about grown-ups; though there have been a number of successful novels for adults that featured children as their leads, be aware that this is a risky decision for a first-time novelist.

If you're writing a young-adult novel, then you read actively in this field and know that these novels are aimed at various age levels, stated in ranges. Your lead should be no older than the top of the range you're targeting.

You should now be able to say, "My lead is a man," "My lead is a woman," "My lead is a _____ -year-old boy" or "My lead is a _____ -year-old girl." Fill in the blanks below:

The genre of the novel I am creating is _____ .

The lead of my novel is a _____ .

❖❖❖

Now that you've got a rudimentary idea of your novel's lead, it's time to throw an event at this character that he'll regard as a crisis.

Coming up with a crisis is the first brainstorming you'll do in the process of creating your novel. To work effectively, a crisis must meet certain criteria. But before you worry about those, let your mind fly free to come up with interesting crisis scenarios, or what I call "Supposes." Use the Suppose List starting on page 37 to jot down crisis ideas whenever they come to you. If you make a conscious effort to look for ideas in all aspects of your life, you'll find that eventually these ideas will start occurring to you on their own. "Where do you get your ideas?" readers often ask novelists. "From everywhere," you'll respond, or "They just come to me!"

Here are some excellent sources of Supposes:

- Your own life
- Relatives
- Friends
- Co-workers
- Television
- Movies
- Radio
- Books
- Newspapers
- Magazines
- The Internet
- Travel
- Dreams
- Eavesdropping
- People watching

The Three Suppose Questions

You must now select the one crisis idea, or Suppose, that appeals to you the most, whatever the reason. It is this Suppose that you will subject to three questions to ensure that that it will work effectively for your novel.

Suppose Question #1: Is This Crisis Appropriate for My Novel's Target Genre?

Based on your reading, you should be able to judge whether this is the kind of crisis that is likely to be presented to the lead of this kind of

Suppose List

Suppose_____

_____

Suppose_____

_____

Suppose_____

_____

Suppose_____

_____

Suppose_____

_____

Suppose_____

_____

Suppose_____

_____

Suppose_____

_____

Suppose_____

_____

Suppose_____

_____

Suppose_____

_____

novel. Let's say, for example, that your target genre is serial-killer thriller. Would "Suppose a woman arrives home one night to find that her house has burned down" work? At face value, no. But with a bit of tweaking, it could work: "Suppose a woman arrives home to find that her house has burned down, killing her young son and his baby-sitter. The police discover evidence that points to the fire's having been started by a serial killer whose murder method is arson." This Suppose would even work if you note that later it will be discovered that the fire is the work of a serial killer.

Or you're writing a horror novel. Would "Suppose a woman fell in love with the son of her father's worst enemy" work? No. This Suppose, at face value, has nothing to do with the kinds of story elements commonly found in horror novels; you would know this from your reading program. How about "A woman finds her husband dead, the number 666 seared into his forehead"? Yes, that could work; the writer clearly has in mind some connection with Satan, of whom many believe the number 666 is a symbol.

Suppose Question #2: Would This Crisis Upset Your Lead's Life in Such a Way That He or She Would Have No Choice But to Try to Set Things Right Again?

A crisis must truly be a crisis, a negative event that turns the lead's life upside down. The crisis must be "bad" enough not only that the lead would have to go after a goal that, once achieved, will set things right again, but also that it could conceivably take the lead the entire length of a novel to achieve this goal.

Consider this Suppose: "A twelve-year-old girl is teased by her classmates about her pink T-shirt." Most people would find it difficult to believe that this event could turn a girl's life upside down to such a degree that she would be forced to seek a goal to set her life right again, to stop the teasing. If the teasing really bothers her, she can stop wearing the T-shirt, or speak to a teacher or the school principal. But even these goals would not take a book's length to achieve. This girl's problem just isn't bad enough.

What about "A twelve-year-old girl is ridiculed by her classmates because her mother, an alcoholic, arrived inebriated at a school play and made a terrible and highly visible scene"? This is more like it. This problem is clearly worse, and it is not as easily solved. It certainly turns the girl's life upside down in a negative way, and to restore her reputation and good relationships at school, she'll no doubt have to seek a goal to solve the crisis—perhaps helping her mother get help for her alcoholism.

Suppose Question #3: Is This Suppose Idea Interesting?

Obviously, we all have different ideas of what's interesting. A book whose premise one person finds intriguing may hold no interest for someone else. But there are ways to gauge an idea's "interest factor."

First of all, and most importantly, does it interest *you*? Would you want to read a book in which the lead was presented with this crisis? If the answer is "No," you'd better select another Suppose idea, or dream up some new ones. Never undertake a novel whose story idea doesn't excite you. This lack of excitement inevitably shows in the writing itself.

Second, from your reading: Is this the kind of idea that has fueled the most interesting and compelling novels in your target genre? In other words, do you think it would interest other people—namely, your readers?

Be careful here. You don't want an idea that is in any way the same as an idea you've already read. The operative word above is *kind*. You want an idea you could conceive of finding in a book in your target genre. It must be, to the best of your knowledge and ability, fresh and original. It should not be an idea, or anything like an idea, you've seen in any other book, or for that matter, seen in a film. Idea theft is not only morally wrong and illegal, it's also likely to get your manuscript rejected. You'll find more on freshness of story ideas in the following chapter.

When you have arrived at a Suppose that meets all of the above criteria, write it below:

Suppose_____

_____

CHAPTER 6

Story Ideas—
Hollywood Style

Every novelist dreams of seeing her story on the big screen, or perhaps on the TV screen. For your novel to be of interest to Hollywood, it must satisfy certain criteria. But even if your novels never make it to the screenplay or teleplay stage, you'll still be giving your readers a bonus if you incorporate—at your discretion, according to the nature of your story—these film/TV criteria. You can use the techniques that make movies work to make your novels work even better.

The overused, even passé term that Hollywood began using in the eighties to describe the most commercial story ideas is "high concept." What does it mean? That's a question my clients ask me all the time.

Over the course of the years I have been an editor, packager and agent. Certain novels I have worked with have drawn film and television people to want to option (or buy the exclusive right to purchase film or TV rights to) them. Some of these optioned novels have even become feature and TV films—an occurrence that is actually rare among optioned works.

I have made observations about the nature of the books I've worked with that have drawn Hollywood interest. These observations can help you as you devise the ideas for your novels.

A High-Impact Story Idea

Your story idea should be so intriguing and compelling in and of itself that its premise, its "hook," will immediately grab the reader's attention. In Hollywood, this refers to the story line alone, without regard to which actors might be cast in it, what the reviews have said or what the word of mouth on the story has been.

Perform a test on your story idea, stating it in the following format:

My novel is a story about a ————————————

who wants to ————————————

——————————————— .

Now, regard this sentence as objectively and dispassionately as you possibly can. Do you believe this story line alone is enough to make people want to buy your novel—without knowing who wrote it, whether it's your first novel or your twelfth, who published it, what the reviews say, or whether it's on any best-seller lists? If the answer is "yes," you've got a high-concept story line, the kind Hollywood likes best.

Quite often, a high-concept novel is one whose title or advertisements convey that the story contains hard-hitting, perennially popular elements; some examples are sex, violence or a controversial subject.

Fresh Yet Familiar

In chapter five we discussed making your Suppose interesting, making it fresh and original yet the kind of idea readers expect to find in your target genre. To give your story the Hollywood touch, you must make certain you've satisfied this criterion. You must come up with a story that will be "comfortable" to your genre's readers, yet will strike them as fresh and new within their genre expectations. How do you do this? The most common method is to take an element that is familiar to your genre's readers, then either twist it in a totally new way or combine it with an element that has never been seen before.

Here's an example. Your target genre is time travel romance, and you know from reading in this subgenre that traditionally the lead—the romance's "heroine"—travels back in time by means of some paranormal device. There she encounters the romance's "hero" (the character we'll later call the romantic involvement), who she ultimately comes to realize is her soul mate, and with whom she remains, thereby proving that love knows no boundaries, not even time.

Invariably, the hero is a man of the past time to which the heroine has time-traveled. But what if he, like the heroine, had come from the future—perhaps by means of the same time travel device the heroine used? Now neither of them can return to the future . . . or perhaps one of them knows how and isn't telling the other, for reasons you'll devise. The idea of two people falling in love, overcoming obstacles to their being together, in an alien time is fresh; the rest of the story meets genre expectations and will therefore be comfortable for the reader. Fresh . . . yet familiar.

A few words of caution. When you twist a familiar story idea, twist it in a way that is truly compelling and interesting. If you combine a familiar story element with a wholly new one, make sure the new one possesses these same qualities. A twist or change alone isn't enough.

It Could Happen to Us

An element common to the majority of high-concept story ideas is that they are set in a time and place with which most people can identify. Readers (and viewers) are able to think as they turn the pages or watch the screen, "This could be me; this could happen to me."

Consider, for instance, stories that place ordinary people in dangerous situations. In Alfred Hitchcock's classic film *North by Northwest*, made from a masterful script by Ernest Lehman, Cary Grant plays Roger Thornhill, an advertising executive mistaken by enemy spies for a U.S. undercover agent named George Kaplan. The entire premise for this clever story idea is set up in a split second: A waiter pages a man named George Kaplan at the exact moment Thornhill summons the waiter; thus Thornhill is mistaken for Kaplan, and as a result his life is turned upside down. An average man becomes embroiled in deadly espionage, culminating with the famous cliff-hanger finale atop the stone faces of Mount Rushmore. He even "gets the girl," played by Eva Marie Saint.

Judith Guest's novel *Ordinary People* appealed to large numbers of readers—and placed this author's first published attempt on national best-seller lists—largely because it dealt with the kinds of trauma and tragedy that commonly plague ordinary people. Most of us could identify with at least one member of the repressed and dysfunctional Jarrett family.

A publishing trend that illustrates this principle was the relatively short-lived popularity of "glitz and glamour" novels in the eighties. In the years prior to the emergence of this genre, novels had for the most part dealt with average people. In the extravagant, materialistic eighties, where anything seemed attainable and people strove for money and all its trappings, books about movie stars and the jet set appealed to those who wanted a taste of the life they aspired to.

At the end of the eighties, as the economy changed and people adopted a more conservative approach to life—indeed, a more simplistic, spiritual approach—this all changed. Publishers saw the decline of the glitz-and-glamour novel in favor of more "down-home" stories—stories about everyday people from all walks of life. Today, most of the novels that hit best-seller lists are about people just like us or sometimes in worse shape than we are.

In her immensely popular novel *Where the Heart Is*, Billie Letts tells the story of pregnant, overweight Novalee Nation, who on her way to Bakersfield, California, is abandoned by her ne'er-do-well boyfriend in an Oklahoma Wal-Mart. Bret Lott's *Jewel* is about Jewel Hilburn, who in World War II–era Mississippi, bears a child with Down's syndrome. These are just two among countless examples of novels that draw on instantly recognizable situations faced by everyday people.

American readers have in fact grown increasingly insular in their reading tastes over recent years. Whereas thrillers set in foreign countries were once quite popular, today American readers are primarily interested in reading stories set mostly if not entirely in the United States. Patricia Highsmith's novel *The Talented Mr. Ripley* is set in 1950s Italy, but its characters are transplanted Americans. And though the story places its lead, Tom Ripley, in contact with people of wealth and privilege, Tom himself starts out quite impoverished, living in a dismal New York apartment, barely making a living. (Note, however, that he is the classic antihero: an amoral serial killer, motivated by his covetousness of the rich life. The talented Highsmith was able to make us care about what happened to this character. In the hands of a less accomplished novelist, this may not have been the case.)

When the historical romance first gained widespread popularity in the 1970s, readers enjoyed stories set not only in America but in exotic locales such as India, Japan and ancient Egypt. As of this writing, publishers are with few exceptions interested only in stories set in America, England, Scotland and Ireland. Moreover, the story's hero or heroine must be American. Back in the seventies, historical romances could be set in virtually any time period. Today editors advise writers to set their stories between 1066, the year of the Norman Conquest, and 1900.

Confining your story's time and place to the familiar produces another benefit in terms of your novel's chances in Hollywood. "Period pieces" and stories set in exotic foreign locales are more expensive to produce, so it follows that the more expensive your story would be to produce, the more difficult it would be to get it optioned or purchased for film adaptation. Other elements that make a story expensive to film are an inordinately large cast of characters, extravagant events that would translate into expensive special effects and lots of inclement weather.

These are, of course, general guidelines. I don't mean to suggest that your novel should follow them all. But if your story would work just as well within them, why not follow them and increase your novel's cinematic odds?

Making the Connection

In addition to familiarity of time and place, readers—and viewers—are drawn to stories that speak to them, stories with which they can make an emotional connection. The ideas behind these stories have a universal appeal.

A story might portray a character having an experience we'd all like to have. For example, tales of the "underdog" triumphing over adversity are perennially popular. The *Rocky* movies are excellent examples; two others are *Norma Rae*, for which Sally Field won an Oscar for her portrayal of a naive textile worker who stands up for workers' rights and wins, and *Erin Brockovich*, in which Julia Roberts plays a file clerk in a small law firm who, through sheer determination, helps her boss win the largest settlement ever paid in a direct-action suit.

A sometimes related and equally audience-pleasing kind of story is that which portrays the triumph of the human spirit. Steven Spielberg recognized this element in Alice Walker's novel *The Color Purple* and turned it into an enormously popular film. David Lean saw the same theme in E.M. Forster's classic novel *A Passage to India*, which he would turn into his last movie.

Predict the Future

Many films succeed because they tie into current trends or timely social topics. Achieving this connection is not as easy as it may sound. Films often take years to make. A novel on which a film might be based could also take several years in its progression from manuscript to finished book.

So how do these novelists do it? By predicting the future—anticipating trends. It's not something everyone can do. It takes a certain kind of intuition and a lot of reading books (fiction and nonfiction), magazines and newspapers; watching TV; going to films and plays; listening to the radio; talking to people . . . . In other words, you must plug yourself into popular culture so that when a new trend or pattern begins to emerge or shows signs that it will, you'll catch it. Movie studios have research departments to predict and identify audience tastes; become your own research department as you weigh story ideas for your novels.

The novelist's job is actually more difficult than the filmmaker's. The novelist must not only identify a coming trend that may not have arrived yet, but he must also write a novel that will attract and entertain readers in the meantime.

Sometimes it's clear a trend that's already here will stick around awhile. At this writing, for example, professional wrestling has been enjoying record popularity for the past several years and shows no signs of flagging. A film called *Ready to Rumble*, aimed at wrestling fans, is not based on a novel, but it could have been. Most likely there are wrestling novels in the works now—novels that will find their way to the big screen.

Another subject pop culture sharpies saw coming was stock car racing. Several series of novels are now available for fans of this sport, and one if not more of these is sure to attract Hollywood interest.

Watch also for trends in *types* of movies. Back in the seventies, the disaster film was all the rage. Viewers watched characters on the screen fight to survive earthquakes, skyscraper fires, massive train wrecks and ocean liners overturned by tidal waves. It wasn't long before a spate of disaster novels appeared; many of them found their way to the screen. And the disaster novels and movies keep coming to this day. In the late nineties, Steve Alten published *Meg*, about a twenty-ton prehistoric shark. Meanwhile, on screen, we watched people run from erupting volcanoes and try to predict devastating tornadoes.

Often one highly successful movie starts a chain of similar movies. Once Hollywood saw how much we loved being terrified by a marauding great white shark, it wasn't long before we were being scared out of our wits by killer whales, giant squids and massive desert snakes. In this case, too, novelists joined in, and an army of monster novels appeared, many of which garnered their authors big Hollywood bucks.

Starting on page 47 you'll find a Trends Journal, pages on which you can record ideas you get about trends and subjects you see growing in popularity. Clip articles from magazines and newspapers that tie into these trends, and paste them onto these pages as well.

Screen Appeal

You can see why high-concept story lines appeal to film and television studios and producers. In this era of sky-high fees for top actors, not to mention staggering budgets for lavishly mounted productions, the notion of making a film that will attract an audience solely through its story line is often not preferable but necessary.

It's on the strength of high concept that many low-budget independent films achieve mammoth success. Usually we recognize none of the actors (though many of them go on to stardom), and the production values are modest. But these films tell one heck of a good story. In the end, that's what film audiences—and novel readers—want most.

Does your story idea have the Hollywood touch? If it doesn't and you can't think of a way to change it so that it does, don't worry about it. But if you *can* think of a way to give your concept that cinematic spark, and doing so won't compromise the story you want to tell, what have you got to lose? Nothing. On the other hand, you'll have a lot to gain.

Trends Journal

Ideas

Trends Journal

Clippings

CHAPTER 7

The Story Goal—Your Novel's Engine

You now have a crisis that's appropriate to your target genre, "bad" enough to make the lead want to pursue a goal to solve it and inherently interesting. Just what goal will your lead devise to set life right side up again?

The Lead's Quest

As you devise this goal for your lead, keep the following important points in mind:

- The goal your lead sets to solve the crisis must be the most logical goal she would set under the circumstances.
- It must be believable that achievement of this goal would solve the crisis.
- This goal must cause your lead to try to gain either possession of something (for example, a person, a thing or information) or relief from something (for example, pain, suffering, fear, oppression, loneliness, domination or poverty).
- It must be clear that if your lead fails to achieve this goal, he will suffer terrible consequences. Life without the crisis solved would be unthinkable.
- Your lead must have a worthy motivation for pursuing this goal. It's not enough that your lead is pursuing this goal to solve the crisis; she must be acting out of a worthy motivation, any of the motivations that drive the heroes in our most compelling stories. Some worthy motivations are duty, love, honor, justice, dignity, integrity, patriotism, redemption and self-respect.
- "Soft" motivations like kindness or generosity don't work as effectively as the "harder" ones just mentioned, because soft emotions do

not usually bring about dramatic, exciting action. For a different reason, negative motivations, such as envy, lust, anger, greed, hatred, vengeance, covetousness and excessive pride, do not work either. We find stories whose leads are driven by such motivations, but because it's far more difficult to make a reader sympathize with an antihero lead of this kind, the beginning novelist should avoid such a story.

• The goal must pit your lead against great odds. It should seem virtually impossible for the lead to achieve this goal.

On page 51 you'll find the Story Idea Worksheet. You may want to photocopy it so you can reuse it. You'll find it's an easy way to test your various notions as you conceive them, then you can pull them together into story ideas.

Story Idea Worksheet

The genre of the novel I am creating is _____

The lead of my novel is a [male/female] [adult/teen/preteen] (circle one).

Suppose [he/she] (circle one)_____

_____

_____

_____

CRISIS CHECKLIST:

☐ Appropriate for target genre?

☐ Will upset lead's life enough so that he/she must try to solve it?

☐ Interesting to you?

☐ Interesting to readers, in your best judgment?

☐ Fresh and original, to the best of your knowledge?

In response to the crisis, my lead decides to _____

_____

_____

_____

_____

GOAL CHECKLIST:

☐ Most logical under the circumstances?

☐ Believable that achievement of this goal will solve the crisis?

☐ Will cause lead to try to gain possession or relief?

☐ If lead fails, he/she will suffer terrible consequences?

☐ Life without achieving this goal and solving the crisis would be unthinkable?

☐ Worthy, high-minded motivation?

☐ Pits lead against great odds?

When all the previous criteria have been satisfied, express your story idea in the following format:

STORY IDEA:

In my novel, whose genre is _____ ,
(GENRE OR SUBGENRE)

the lead, a _____
        (MALE/FEMALE),   (ADULT/TEEN/PRETEEN),   (CRISIS)

_____

_____

_____

_____

_____

_____

_____

_____

As a result, my lead decides to _____
                                            (GOAL)

_____

_____

_____

_____

_____

_____

_____

_____

_____

CHAPTER 8

Research: When and How Much?

Why a chapter on research? Because research affects the writing process in a number of important ways—some of them are undesirable.

When does research become a bad thing? When writers use it as an excuse not to start writing yet. I've seen writers spend ten years researching a novel that not only didn't require such exhaustive background work; it would have been better off without it. Still other writers love doing research so much—or at least they say they do—that they never write at all. It's like being a perpetual student, staying in school and earning degree after degree to put off venturing out into the real world.

Research has its rightful place in the novel writing process and is in fact vital to many kinds of stories. The keys to keeping it under control are to understand that there are two kinds of research for the novelist; know which kind should be done when and know when not to do research at all.

Background Research

The first kind of research, the kind in which some writers mire themselves as a means of putting off actually writing, is background research. Background research is exactly what it sounds like: investigating an era, a subject, an industry or whatever is necessary to come up with a believable plot for your novel.

Background research is necessary when you have an idea for a novel that is either set in an unfamiliar time or place or is about a subject that you know so little about, you can't even begin to construct a story until you know more.

Imagine, for example, a writer with an idea for a novel set in the field of nature preservation. His lead is a forest ranger. Though he has the vaguest notion of an idea—the beginnings of a Suppose—he hasn't a notion of exactly what forest rangers *do* all day. And he must know this before he can start putting a story together, before he can start stringing actions together for his lead.

This chapter isn't about how to research. You know what the various methods are, from consulting books and other written materials in libraries to surfing the Net to conducting informational interviews. This chapter is about *how much* background research to do.

How can you avoid falling into the perpetual-research trap, yet still learn enough to work with? By setting out concrete questions for yourself before you even begin. In most cases the writers who mire themselves in research and never get to the novel itself use what I call the "immersion approach." They read book after book, fill notebook upon notebook with notes, in an effort to insert themselves as deeply as possible into their subject. There is no real plan to their work—all books on the subject are fair game; it's impossible to go too deep; no detail is unimportant. It's all in the name of immersion.

If, on the other hand, you force yourself to compile a list of questions you need answers to before you can build your story, you've already gone a long way toward limiting the research phase.

Let's take our forest ranger example. Our hypothetical writer has a vague notion for a thriller set in the world of nature conservation; his Suppose is "Suppose a man [the forest ranger] discovered that his best friend, a fellow ranger, was murdering animals and selling their [?] on the black market."

Our writer must ask himself what *basic* information he needs to begin devising his story. Here are some likely questions:

- What animal products are sold on the black market? (Fur, skin, tusks, etc.)
- Around which of these products is there likeliest to be violence/danger?
- In what countries does this selling occur?
- Are the animals that provide these products protected? Where? (Protected forests, jungles, savannas, etc.)
- What are the people called whose job it is to protect these places?

- What are these people's primary activities in performing their jobs?
- Do these people work from any sort of headquarters on or near the land they protect, or do they move about, with no central headquarters?
- If they do work from a headquarters, where would it be?
- What would it be like? (Building, cabin, tower, etc.)
- How many people would work in one facility? On one protected area? Are there shifts so that protection is constant?
- If there is more than one person, how do they communicate?

And so on. Questions lead to more questions. When the actual research begins, yet more questions inevitably arise. But the research process has been shaped into a finite project. Each question is tackled, one at a time, and when it's answered, the novelist moves on to the next one. If the novelist resists the temptation to be sidetracked, which can lead to dangerous immersion, then the background research process has a definite end, and the plotting phase can begin.

When Not to Do Background Research

More than once I have advised a writer faced with extensive background research to reconsider her project entirely. In these instances it was clear that although the writer had a strong interest in the subject she was about to research, her absolute lack of knowledge of this subject made research impractical; the learning curve was too steep. To conduct the research necessary to achieve even a rudimentary knowledge of the subject would take so long that by the time the book itself was written, too much time would have passed, causing too long a time span. Publishers want books good *and* fast—usually no more than a year apart. In terms of career strategy, sometimes a project simply isn't practical.

When I decided to write my own fiction, I knew I would write cozy mysteries, because what I most enjoy reading is cozy mysteries, both contemporary and historical. I was torn, however, between two ideas.

One idea was to write a series featuring a sleuth who was a literary agent in a present-day New Jersey village and who was helped in her detecting by her cat. The other was to feature as my detective an alchemist in medieval London. On reflection, I realized that despite my extensive reading of novels set in the medieval period, I would have an enormous amount of research to do—research that would probably have to be added to for each novel in my series.

On the other hand, I *am* a literary agent, I live in a small New Jersey town and a number of cats have owned me. For this idea, there would be no learning curve at all. Because I'm an agent, making my living selling books, when it comes to decisions such as this I'm practical if nothing else. My choice was clear. I would follow the age-old adage "Write what you know." Thus, Jane Stuart and Winky of Shady Hills, New Jersey, were born.

Think hard about any project you're considering that will require too long a research period. Sometimes, in terms of your career, the learning curve is just too steep.

Spot Research

The other kind of research is what I call spot research. It's the small piece of information you need at a precise moment in the plotting or writing of your novel. What's the actual name of rat poison? What kind of wood would that table likely be made of? What's a town about fifteen miles south of Stamford, Connecticut?

As with background research, writers often use an item of spot research as an excuse to stop plotting or writing and start searching. Entire days can be spent looking for a tiny item of information—days that will likely spoil the flow and momentum of your work.

Items that require spot research are items that matter but can wait until you're done. When you're plotting or writing your novel and one of these items arises, don't stop; signify that you'll have to research this later by typing "[????]" or "TO COME" or the old journalist's expression, "tk" (*to come*). At the same time, jot on a piece of paper that you've headed "Research" and place it near your keyboard. Thus, in your manuscript you type:

> If Gail had headed south on Route 17, she'd definitely have
> passed through Paramus and then [????].

And on your Research sheet you write:

Town south of Paramus.

When I'm plotting or writing a novel, I force myself never to stop to do spot research. I do all of that when my first draft is completed and printed out. Since I don't let myself stop to research, I have no excuse to stop writing. I counsel the novelists I represent, especially the ones on tight deadlines, to follow this practice, and I counsel you to do the same.

PART III

Your Story People

CHAPTER 9

The Lead

So far you may have only the most basic idea of who your novel's lead is—male or female, adult, teen or preteen. Now it's time to carefully define this character, the most important of all the characters in your novel—the "star" of your story.

To begin with, review the Story Idea from the end of your Story Idea Worksheet on page 52.

The Lead's Character Fact List

On the Lead's Character Fact List starting on page 69, record the decisions you make about your novel's lead character, from his appearance to how he lives and works to his strengths and weaknesses.

The Lead's Character Fact List (like all of your major characters' fact lists) includes a Writing Coach column to remind you of the most important factors to consider as you make decisions about your lead. Most of the traits are also keyed to more detailed instructions, which you'll find directly after the Lead's Character Fact List.

1. Age

Begin with what you entered in your Story Idea Worksheet on page 51 (adult, teen or preteen) and specify more exactly.

Questions to ask in deciding your lead's age:

• **Does your Suppose suggest your lead's age?** For example, if your Suppose was "Suppose the CEO of a major computer company learned that a group of his employees were running a global hacker ring, infiltrating the world's top government agencies," you would want to make your lead old enough that it would be believable that he could have attained this position in his company. If your Suppose was "Suppose a woman's college freshman son was accused of rape," your lead could conceivably be in her late forties, if she had given birth to him when she was thirty. (Note: Sometimes at this stage it's not yet possible to arrive at an exact age for your lead, though an age range may be possible. If the latter is the case, state this range on your fact list, knowing that decisions you make later about your lead will help you be more specific here.)

• **Does your target genre suggest your lead's age?** If you're writing a novel for teens or preteens, your lead should be the age of your oldest target reader. If you're writing a romance targeted at a specific publisher's line (Silhouette, Harlequin, etc.), consult the publisher's tip sheet (see page 24) for age requirements. If you're writing a book about a young man who is a member of Generation X—a child of the eighties—your lead could (at the time of this book's publication) be twenty or twenty-one. If you're writing a "mature romance," your lead might be in her late forties or early fifties (see previous note about age ranges).

2. Physical

You have thus far established your lead's gender and age, which will begin to suggest an appearance. Now consider your Suppose for further cues.

Questions to ask in determining your lead's physical appearance:

• **Does your lead's ethnic background suggest anything specific in terms of appearance?** You may already have decided that your novel will feature an African-American woman or a Japanese man.

• **Does the Suppose itself suggest an appearance?** Will you be writing about a Wall Street yuppie? A Forty-Second Street prostitute? A person who is plain and quiet?

• **Does your target genre suggest an appearance?** The lead of a historical romance should be a beautiful woman. If you're writing a senior-sleuth cozy mystery, you might want your lead to be in her sixties or seventies.

• **Do you already have a mental picture of your lead?** It's quite common for a novelist to simply *know* what her lead looks like. This phenomenon shouldn't be ignored, because it's when we can clearly envision a character that we write most convincingly about him or her.

The Character Photo Collage

Before supplying the specific data pertaining to your lead's body type, height, hair color and eye color, make use of a technique used by many veteran novelists—creating a Character Photo Collage. Gather as many magazines and mail-order catalogs as you can find and, keeping the answers to the previous questions in mind, look for a color photograph of a person who looks as if he or she might fit the role of your lead. When you come upon a likely candidate, consider whether you can imagine this person as your lead. Can you imagine this person speaking to and interacting with other characters? Reacting to the crisis of your Suppose?

Don't settle for the first possible photo you find. Keep looking until you find someone you feel comfortable with, someone who really fits the part. When you have selected the best of the possibilities, cut out the photo and tape or paste it onto the Lead's Photo Collage on pages 74–75. Keep in mind that catalogs and magazines frequently run multiple pictures of the same person modeling different clothes and doing different things in different settings. Look for such additional photos and clip these out as well, pasting them onto the collage. (Later, if you spot more photos of this person in new catalogs or magazines, add them to the page.)

Now, with your Lead's Photo Collage before you, supply the appearance details on your Lead's Character Fact List.

3. Mannerisms

Using your writer's imagination, study your Lead's Photo Collage and picture this character speaking, listening, moving, laughing, eating, expressing anger. Concentrate—keep studying the collage—until you can envision this person in action. What do you see? How would you describe this character's manner? What would be the most distinctive trait?

Is this person calm and cool in most situations, or hotheaded, perhaps using exaggerated facial expressions? Is this person loud or subdued? Forceful or meek? Does this character have an easy smile, or is she guarded, wary? Is a frown his usual expression? How does this character use her hands? When speaking, does he gesticulate animatedly? Turn her head in sharp, sudden movements? Or are this character's mannerisms more fluid, languid? Is this a person who never moves quickly or sharply for anyone or anything?

Don't forget the eyes. My book *Eye Language* is about how our eyes express our feelings and true desires. Does this character stare a lot? Slide sly glances? Look away shyly? Open his eyes wide when happy, excited or surprised? Does she use a lot of "eye cutoffs," gestures in which the eyelids close or "stammer" because she must shut out excessive stimuli, or because she can't bear to meet other people's gaze?

Move down the body. Perhaps this character is agile and lithe, able to move quickly and easily. Or is he stiff and slow moving?

What about the legs? If this is a nervous person, she might have trouble standing still. Does he pace a lot? Tap her feet? Stomp one foot when angry?

These are examples of the many ways in which people express themselves through their mannerisms.

4. Distinctive Speech Pattern

Imagine your lead in action, this time speaking.

Who your lead is will largely determine how he speaks. You may already have decided who your lead is when you devised your story idea. A scientist speaks differently from a teenager; a lawyer speaks differently from an inner-city gang member; a seventeenth-century sea captain speaks differently from a Roman centurion.

Does this character, in your mind's eye, possess any special qualities with respect to the way she speaks? To begin with, is this a careful speaker who weighs and measures every word, a reckless talker who immediately releases whatever pops into his head, or something in between? Is this person careful not to offend others or liberal in the use of profanity? Is he careful most of the time, but unable to curb his cursing in times of great stress?

Does this person tend to use a lot of hyperbole—is everything "the best," "the biggest" or "the greatest"? Or does she downplay most things, so that her distinctive speech pattern is to be subdued, calm?

Does this character commit a lot of malapropisms? Fall back on clichés? Mix metaphors? Use a lot of long words?

Does he have a favorite expression (for example, saying, "Y'know what I mean?" after practically every sentence, or addressing all women as "honey")?

Is this character educated and therefore well-spoken, or does she make a lot of grammatical errors?

5. Personality

Here, too, you must combine any clues to personality you've drawn from your lead as you've defined him or her thus far with any you imagine when you study the Lead's Photo Collage. There are no restrictions on the number and kind of qualities you imagine this character having. Jot down any that occur to you, for example, "Funny, able to laugh at himself; self-deprecating" or "Intense, driven, usually serious."

However, there are four qualities that you *must* give your lead. These qualities will ensure that your reader likes and respects your lead and therefore cares whether your lead succeeds or fails in her quest to achieve the story goal. It is vital that your reader care deeply about your lead and his mission. Books that don't arouse these feelings in readers are books readers stop reading halfway through—books that arouse no desire in the reader to pick up another of this author's books. Obviously, you can't let this happen.

The four qualities that follow are the classic traits shared by the heroes and heroines of stories from as long as people have *told* stories. Combined, they are responsible for making a story's lead bigger than life, able to rise above adversity in ways many of us wouldn't be capable of doing.

Likability

This one may seem obvious, yet new writers frequently overlook or ignore it. Your lead must simply be someone we like, someone we want to spend time with. What makes a character likable? To start with, she should have a good sense of humor and be able to laugh at herself; she shouldn't always take herself too seriously. Though your lead will have admirable qualities, she must be modest about them, though not falsely so. Your lead must be a kind, considerate person who is concerned about the welfare and well-being of others.

Competence

Your lead should be accomplished at the basic living of life. This means he is a sensible, reasonably intelligent person. He will make frequent use of these two qualities when confronting problems and obstacles that stand in the way of achieving the story goal. Though your lead needn't necessarily be extraordinarily clever or shrewd, he must possess a healthy share of good old common sense.

Virtue

This trait is highly important. Your lead must be a virtuous, moral person who knows right from wrong, good from evil. This is not to say that this character must be a saint. She is, after all, only human, capable of making moral mistakes just like anyone else. She won't always take the high road. But later, if she has done something illegal, unethical or immoral, she will be aware of it and will seek to make reparation for it.

Courage

This is your lead's most important trait of all. He must possess a core of inner strength that will enable him to face and deal with the toughest of the obstacles that will arise as he strives to attain the story goal. Your lead's courage needn't be a conspicuous quality. It may be hidden, residing quietly within him, ready to be drawn upon when needed. Your lead may falter at times before pulling himself up again to fight.

6. Background

Your lead's background is her life up to now, the time of your story. To create this background, you must draw cues and clues from your Suppose, from the ways in which you've defined your lead thus far and from more imaginative study of your Lead's Photo Collage.

In creating a background for your lead, it isn't necessary to go into exhaustive detail. Select facts and events that would have been the most important in your lead's development. You will inevitably fill out details of your lead's past life as you need them in the actual writing of your novel.

Here are some areas to consider as you build a past for your lead.

Geography

Where was he born? Where did he grow up? Was he raised in one place, or did his family move around?

Childhood

What was your lead's childhood like? Was she happy, popular, well adjusted? Miserable, sometimes unhappy, lonely, out of place? Why? A joiner? An outsider?

Family

What were your lead's parents like? Does he have any siblings? Was he close to any of them? Was your lead the oldest child? Youngest? Middle? An only child? What about childhood friends? Were any especially important? Did your lead marry? Have any children?

Education/Vocation

Did she go to college? If so, where? Did she do graduate work? If so, in what field? Did she receive any other kind of education or training? What is her work history?

7. Personal Life

This is your lead's life when she isn't working. Build this life on your lead's life as you've defined it so far, and use your writer's imagination when necessary to fill in any gaps.

Where does your lead live? In a house, an apartment, a co-op or condominium?

In what state or country? In what city or town (real or fictitious)? In what area, on what street?

Does your lead live alone, or is there someone else at home? Is he single? Married? Does he live with someone he isn't married to—a partner, a parent? Are there children? If so, how many? What are their names and ages? Are there any pets?

Consider your lead's social life. Who are her closest friends? Her friends in general? In what kinds of circles does she socialize? Who is her best friend? It could be someone at work (though you'll go into that in greater detail when you define your lead's work life). What does she do with these friends?

What does your lead do in his free or leisure time? Is he an outdoors kind of person who enjoys sports or vigorous activities such as hiking or camping? Or is he perfectly content cooking for a few friends and then watching a video? Consider fitness activities, cultural pursuits and activities involving children.

8. Private Life

Your lead's private life is what she does when she's alone. Make inferences from your lead's life as you have defined it thus far, and use your imagination to fill in the blanks. Contemplate your Lead's Photo Collage for inspiration.

What are your lead's hobbies? Interests? Does she have a personal passion—painting, music, antiques, gardening, traveling, reading?

9. Work Life

Chances are you've already made decisions about your lead's work life, the way he earns a living. If not, build now on what you've decided so far; make inferences from the life you've already created for him.

How does your lead earn a livelihood? Is she employed or self-employed? Does she work in an office—if so, where, and what is it like?—or at home? Who are her co-workers, if any? Whom does she report to? Who reports to her? Who does she consider her allies at work? Her rivals?

10. Strength

By this time you have a pretty clear picture of your lead's personality—one you have created for him. Based on how you have defined this character, what would you say is his strongest positive trait? Your lead has numerous positive traits, but which one—other than likability, competence, virtue and courage—stands out most visibly? Possible strengths are fairness, ingenuity, discretion, adaptability, humor, loyalty, kindness, tolerance, generosity and resourcefulness.

11. Weakness

Based on how you have defined this character, what would you imagine to be her strongest negative trait, her fatal flaw? Some possibilities are envy, greed, vanity, laziness, arrogance, insecurity, narcissism, intolerance, conceitedness, false pride, excess generosity and low self-esteem.

12. Name

There's a reason this trait comes last on the Character Fact List. Your lead's name must fit him as you've defined his personality. Selecting a name first and then creating a character under it rarely works because then the personality suits the name. For our purposes, personality comes first, evolving as it does from your Suppose and Story Idea.

The key, then, is to select a name that fits this person you've created. Here are some tips for naming your characters.

First, collect as many name sources as you can. These include the most comprehensive baby name book you can find, newspapers, magazines and telephone directories. There's even a name book just for writers that I recommend: *The Writer's Digest Character Naming Sourcebook,* by Sherrilyn Kenyon with Hal Blythe and Charlie Sweet (Writer's Digest Books). It lists thousands of names from various cultures around the world. Surfing the Internet is always helpful for further inspiration.

Now ask yourself the following questions:

• Does the character's background suggest any names or kinds of names?

• Would the character's parents have been likely to select a specific name or kind of name?

• Was the name you're considering in fashion when your character was born?

• Does the name you're considering fit the character's personality? Few of us legally change the names we're given at birth, but many of us alter them to better fit our personalities. We may prefer a more or less formal version or a variation of the name we've been given. For instance, Francis prefers Frank, Dorothy prefers Dot, Elliott James Carter prefers Jim and so on.

• Vary the sound and length of your characters' names. Avoid giving all of your characters simple Anglo names, a common beginner's error.

• Avoid using names that end alike or similarly: Carla and Lola, Ronny and Tommy, Arlene and Eileen, Al and Hal, Anderson and Wolfson.

• Avoid using names ending in *s*. They make for clumsy possessives that readers trip over: Louis's, Moses', the Tobiases'.

• Avoid overly long names, especially for your lead and other major characters. Readers don't want to read Theodore or Francesca or Angelica over and over again, any more than you want to type them.

• To the extent possible, use a different initial for all of your characters' first and last names. Readers may become confused when there's a Robert and a Roger, a Sandra and a Stephanie, a Mr. Tate and a Mr. Thomas. On page 76 you'll find a Character Name Sheet to keep track of the initials you've used as you name your creations. Keep coming back to this sheet as you name each of your characters.

Once you've arrived at a satisfactory name for your lead, enter it on the Lead's Character Fact List (page 73), and write it at the bottom of your Lead's Photo Collage (page 75).

Your lead is now a fully realized character, someone you know well enough to begin moving her through your novel's plot. Before beginning to plot, however, you must create the rest of your novel's major characters: the opposition, the confidant, the romantic involvement (if appropriate) and others. You'll do this in the following chapters.

Lead's Character Fact List

TRAIT	DESCRIPTION	WRITING COACH
Story Goal	To	◀ Take from Story Idea Worksheet, page 52.
Gender		◀ Take from Story Idea Worksheet, page 51.
Age		◀ Take from your Story Idea Worksheet and define more specifically. (1—page 59)
Physical		◀ Gender and age are established. Now look for further clues to appearance in your Suppose. (2—page 60).
Body Type		◀ Consult Lead's Photo Collage. Thin? Svelte? Wiry? Fat? Husky? Stocky? Muscular? Scrawny? Voluptuous?
Height		◀ Consult Lead's Photo Collage. Tall? Medium height? Short? Decide on an exact height.
Hair Color and Style		◀ Consult Lead's Photo Collage. Blond, brown, black (raven), red, auburn, gray, white; light, medium, dark? Short, long, limp, teased, clean, dirty; a specific haircut?

Lead's Character Fact List		
TRAIT	**DESCRIPTION**	**WRITING COACH**
Eye Color		◄ Consult Lead's Photo Collage. Gray, green, blue, violet, brown, deep brown, hazel; a combination?
Mannerisms		◄ Study Lead's Photo Collage and imagine this character in action. What is the most distinctive or noticeable mannerism? (3—page 61)
Distinctive Speech Pattern		◄ Study Lead's Photo Collage and imagine this character speaking. What is the most distinctive feature of his/her way of speaking? (4—page 62)
Personal		
Personality		◄ Draw clues from how you've defined your lead so far, as well as from studying Lead's Photo Collage.
	Likability	◄ *Also*: the four classic traits for all leads. (5—page 63)
	Competence	

Lead's Character Fact List		
TRAIT	**DESCRIPTION**	**WRITING COACH**
	Virtue	
	Courage	
Background		◄ Draw clues from your Suppose, how you've defined your lead so far and studying your Lead's Photo Collage.
	Geography	◄ Areas to explore. (6—page 64)
	Childhood	
	Family	

Lead's Character Fact List

TRAIT	DESCRIPTION	WRITING COACH
	Education/Vocation	
Personal Life		◄ Your lead's life when he or she isn't working. Draw clues from your lead's life as you've defined it thus far. Consider kind of home, who else lives there, social life, leisure pursuits. (7—page 65)
Private Life		◄ Your lead's life when he or she is alone. Draw clues from your lead's life as you've defined it thus far. Consider hobbies and interests. (8—page 66)
Work Life		◄ How your lead earns his or her living. Draw clues from your lead's life as you've defined it thus far. Include type of work, where he or she does it, the people he or she works with. (9—page 66)
Strength		◄ Your lead's strongest positive trait. Review above traits; which positive one stands out most visibly? (10—page 66)

Lead's Character Fact List		
TRAIT	**DESCRIPTION**	**WRITING COACH**
Weakness		◀ Your lead's strongest negative trait. Review above traits; which negative one stands out most visibly? (11—page 66)
Name		◀ Select a name that's appropriate for your lead as you've defined him or her (12—page 66). Record it on Character Name Sheet (page 76).

Lead's Photo Collage

Lead's Photo Collage *(page 2)*

Name: _____

Character Name Sheet

Record your characters' first and last names below.

A   N

B   O

C   P

D   Q

E   R

F   S

G   T

H   U

I   V

J   W

K   X

L   Y

M   Z

CHAPTER 10

The Opposition

The second major character you must define before you can start plotting is the opposition, also sometimes known as the villain or the antagonist. Whatever you call this character, her role in the novel is to serve as the greatest obstacle to the lead achieving the story goal.

Keep the following points in mind as you define your opposition.

The Opposition Must Be a Person

In the Marshall Plan, the opposition is always human. This is the strongest type of opposition to write, the type that comes across most effectively, because nothing stirs readers like person-against-person conflict. The opposition is not an act of God or force of nature, such as a fire, flood, drought, blizzard or earthquake. Nor is it a group of people, such as a gang or corporation or government. Finally, it is not a life condition, such as poverty, corruption or the apathy of society as a whole.

The Opposition Must Be an Equal Match for Your Lead

The best novels pit their lead against an opposition of equal strength. A worthy foe for the lead ensures that the lead will have enough problems attaining the story goal to sustain an entire novel's length. An equal opposition also ensures a good strong fight, which always makes for compelling reading. And an opposition who's an equal match for your lead is believable to readers. When the opposition is clearly an inferior match to the lead, readers wonder why the lead doesn't just achieve the goal and end the story. You don't want this to happen.

What do I mean by an equal match? Equal on the level at which the lead will strive to achieve the story goal. For example, a story about survival in the Arctic, in which the lead must rely on his physical stamina and endurance, means the opposition must be equally matched in this way. A novel whose lead is a shrewd detective on the trail of a serial killer would require that the killer be equal to the detective in terms of cunning. Think first of your lead's special skills and talents that will help her achieve the story goal, then bestow your opposition with a large enough share of the same talents that your lead will be given a real run for her money—a run that will keep readers turning pages.

The Opposition Isn't Necessarily Evil, Just Opposite

Contrary to popular belief, the opposition needn't be an evil person. She may simply be in quest of a goal that directly conflicts with that of the lead, thereby constituting the lead's main impediment.

Take, for example, a woman who loves your lead's boyfriend as much as your lead does. She's not evil, just in love. At the office, a rival for a plum position isn't necessarily wicked, just ambitious.

The Ideal Opposition Is Someone the Lead Already Knows

The reason the ideal opposition is someone already known to the lead is that this is usually how life really works: We find ourselves thwarted in the striving for our goals by a person who's already in our life. Another reason for making the opposition someone already in the lead's life is that then you don't run the risk of creating an opposition who seems to have fallen from the sky for the sole purpose of thwarting your lead—a common mistake among beginners.

Examples of oppositions who already play a role in the lead's life are a co-worker, a spouse or other relative, a friend, a boss or a business rival. In the most effective stories, even if the lead doesn't exactly *know* the opposition, there is usually some tie or connection between the lead and the opposition. For example, they may know someone in common or have a shared event in their past.

The Invisible Opposition

In some types of novels, the opposition is "invisible." In other words, though this character still possesses all of the above traits and is working counter to the lead's attainment of the story goal, the lead does not know who this person is.

One example of an invisible opposition is the killer in a murder mystery. The whole point of this type of novel is to present the reader with a puzzle: Who done it? In the case of this kind of book, the lead's story goal is to deduce the murderer's identity. Thus, the invisible opposition is the whole point of the story.

Another example of an invisible opposition may be found in many suspense novels. Someone is working to harm, frighten or otherwise make life unpleasant for the lead, but the lead does not know who this person is. In the woman-in-jeopardy suspense novel, someone is terrorizing the lead—scary phone calls, poisoned pets, snatched children, you name it—but it's not until the end that this opposition makes himself known to the lead. In the Gothic novel, there are typically two men who become important in the life of the lead: one man who is dark, brooding and inscrutable, another who appears to be benevolent toward the lead. It's not until the end of the story that we learn which man is the opposition; often the one who appeared to be bad isn't really bad at all, but had other, justifiable reasons for his apparent malevolence.

Devising the Most Effective Opposition for Your Lead

Most of the time as you create your stories you'll find that there are at least several good candidates for your lead's opposition. The trick is to settle on the one who will work most effectively.

The search for the best opposition starts in your Story Idea. Reread it on pages 51-52, then use the Opposition Worksheet starting on page 81 to help you brainstorm and arrive at the most effective opposition for your lead.

Inevitably, at least one number will be repeated. This is the number of the character to use as your lead's opposition.

The Opposition's Character Fact List

On the Opposition's Character Fact List starting on page 83, record the decisions you make about your novel's opposition character, the one you selected as a result of your brainstorming with the Opposition Worksheet.

Your opposition is now fully realized—a character for your lead to reckon with in her pursuit of the story goal. With all this opposition, your lead will need someone on her side to talk to and confide in. That's the confidant, whom you'll create in chapter eleven.

Opposition Worksheet

Complete the sentence below, working from your Story Idea on page 52.

My lead's story goal is to _____

_____

_____

Now use the table below to complete the following statement:

Ten possible characters (whether they are people I already have in mind for my story or people I would create) who would realistically have a strong reason to want to prevent my lead from achieving this goal, or have a goal in direct conflict with that of my lead, are:

What would be this character's role in my story?	Would this character be an equal match for my lead?	Why would this character oppose my lead?
Example: Alan's boss at CyberCorp.	Yes—he would be clever and cunning; ruthlessly ambitious.	Because if Alan discovered that the boss has been feeding company secrets to the competition, the boss would be ruined.
1.		
2.		
3.		
4.		

5.		
6.		
7.		
8.		
9.		
10.		

Now study your answers, imagining each possible opposition in action—involved in a heated encounter with your lead—and answer the following questions:

Of all of the above possibilities, the one I imagine would have the greatest
potential for individual direct conflicts with my lead is . . . No. _____

Of all of the above possiblities, the one I find most interesting
as a character is . . .   No. _____

Of all of the above possibilities, the one I think I would
most enjoy writing about is . . .   No. _____

Of all of the above possibilities, the one I think would pose the
greatest obstacle to my lead is . . .   No. _____

Opposition's Character Fact List

TRAIT	DESCRIPTION	WRITING COACH
Story Goal	To	◀ Must be a goal in direct conflict with the lead's attainment of his or her story goal, or to stop the lead from attaining the story goal.
Gender		◀ Take from Opposition Worksheet, page 81.
Age		◀ A likely age, given the confidant's position and place in life, etc.
Physical		◀ Create an Opposition's Photo Collage on page 86.
Body Type		◀ Consult Opposition's Photo Collage. Thin? Svelte? Wiry? Fat? Husky? Stocky? Muscular? Scrawny? Voluptuous?
Height		◀ Consult Opposition's Photo Collage. Tall? Medium height? Short? Decide on an exact height.
Hair Color and Style		◀ Consult Opposition's Photo Collage. Blond, brown, black (raven), red, auburn, gray, white; light, medium, dark? Short, long, limp, teased, clean, dirty; a specific haircut?

Opposition's Character Fact List

TRAIT	DESCRIPTION	WRITING COACH
Eye Color		◀ Consult Opposition's Photo Collage. Gray, green, blue, violet, brown, deep brown, hazel; a combination?
Mannerisms		◀ Study Opposition's Photo Collage and imagine this character in action. What is the most distinctive or noticeable mannerism?
Distinctive Speech Pattern		◀ Study Opposition's Photo Collage and imagine this character speaking. What is the most distinctive feature of his/her way of speaking?
Personal		
Personality		◀ Draw clues from how you've defined your opposition so far, as well as from studying Opposition's Photo Collage.
Background		◀ Draw clues from how you've defined your opposition so far and from studying your Opposition's Photo Collage. Opposition's background needn't be as extensive as for lead.
Personal Life		◀ Your opposition's life when he or she isn't working. Draw clues from your opposition's life as you've defined it thus far. Consider kind of home, who else lives there, social life, leisure pursuits.

Opposition's Character Fact List

TRAIT	DESCRIPTION	WRITING COACH
Private Life		◀ Your opposition's life when he or she is alone. Draw clues from your opposition's life as you've defined it thus far. Consider hobbies and interests.
Work Life		◀ How your opposition earns his or her living. Draw clues from your opposition's life as you've defined it thus far. Include type of work, where he or she does it, the people he or she works with.
Strength		◀ Your opposition's strongest positive trait. Review above traits; which positive one stands out most visibly?
Weakness		◀ Your opposition's strongest negative trait. Review above traits; which negative one stands out most visibly?
Name		◀ Select a name that's appropriate for your opposition as you've defined him or her. See character naming advice on page 66. Enter name at bottom of Opposition's Photo Collage (page 86) and record it on Character Name Sheet.

Opposition's Photo Collage

Name: _____

CHAPTER 11

The Confidant

The third major character to create before you begin the plotting process is the confidant. As you apply my plan for novel writing, you may notice that it includes some elements that aren't found in every novel. The confidant is one of these elements.

The confidant is a character close to the lead—physically and emotionally—with whom the lead shares his innermost fears, secrets and thoughts. As you plot with the Marshall Plan, there will be times when your lead will react strongly to conflicts and obstacles he has encountered. As part of this reaction, the lead will then make a new plan for going forward in his quest to attain the story goal. In the majority of cases, it will be more effective for the lead to have another person there as a sounding board—someone to bounce ideas off of, get advice from, receive encouragement from—than to have the lead undergo this process alone.

Most importantly, the story goal of the confidant is to help the lead achieve her story goal. Though the confidant will sometimes disagree with the lead, will grow impatient and tell her to buck up and be strong, at heart the confidant is completely sympathetic to the lead and her quest.

Though not every novel contains a character who plays this role, most movies do, particularly because a movie is a totally visual medium. To gain audience understanding and sympathy, it's vital to provide a character with whom the lead can openly express feelings and try out ideas for moving forward.

Ideally, the confidant will be a character who already plays some other important role in the lead's life, for example, a spouse or co-worker. A confidant like this is more believable to readers, who scratch their heads and wonder at the confidant who appears to exist only to serve as a listener and advisor to the lead. In most cases, this is exactly true: The author *did* insert this character simply to play this role, and as a result, this aspect of the story feels contrived and unnatural.

Creating the Confidant

Who can play the role of confidant to your lead? The first step in designating this character is to reread your Lead's Character Fact List. Chances are good you have already mentioned the likeliest character to play this part, though maybe not by name.

For instance, you may have said about your lead's work life: "His office is small and intimate—three architects including him and two assistants. He has formed close relationships with the other two architects and considers them his friends." In this case, a good candidate would be one of the other architects.

Or in describing your lead's personal life, you may have written: "She can't afford a place of her own on the salary she earns as an editorial assistant, so for the past year she has been sharing her apartment with a roommate—a languid, good-hearted young woman named Helga." There's another prime choice for confidant, name and all.

To help you in selecting a confidant for your lead, here are some possible roles this character may also play:

administrative assistant
advisor
associate
aunt
auto mechanic
baby-sitter
bank teller
bartender
bookie
boss
brother
card playing pal (poker, bridge, etc.)
child's friend
church friend
classmate
cleaning man or woman

coach
colleague
daughter
drinking friend
father
fellow group member (book group, hobby, religious, etc.)
fraternity brother
friend
game playing pal (mah-jongg, etc.)
gardener
grandfather
grandmother
help line volunteer
husband
instructor
letter carrier

librarian	son
lover	sorority sister
mother	sports pal (golf, tennis, bowling,
neighbor	jogging, etc.)
parent's friend	storekeeper
police officer	student
post office clerk	synagogue friend
prostitute	tailor
pupil	travel agent
repair person	teacher
roommate	trainer
secretary	uncle
servant	waitperson
sister	wife

Almost any sort of person can play the role of confidant. If you haven't found any clues to possible confidants in your Lead's Character Fact List, give some thought now to the kinds of people with whom your lead would naturally come into contact during the course of his day-to-day life. All you need is someone who could believably share intimate conversations with your lead and who is likely to be around a lot.

Selecting the Most Effective Confidant for Your Lead

You'll no doubt come up with at least several characters who could play the role of confidant quite nicely. The key is to pick the one who will work most effectively in your story. Use the Confidant Worksheet starting on page 91 to help you brainstorm and settle on the ideal candidate.

Inevitably, at least one number will be repeated. This is the number of the character to use as your lead's confidant.

The Confidant's Character Fact List

On the Confidant's Character Fact List starting on page 93, record the decisions you make about your book's confidant, whom you selected by means of the Confidant Worksheet.

Your lead's confidant is now a complete character, someone your lead can talk to, confide in and bounce ideas off of.

Sometimes, however, it's appropriate to give your lead more than just someone to talk to. Sometimes your lead needs a love interest, what I call the romantic involvement. In the next chapter you'll decide whether this character is right for the novel you're creating, and if so, you'll bring this person to life.

Confidant Worksheet

Complete the sentence below, working from your Story Idea on page 52.

My lead's story goal is to _____

_____

_____

Now use the table below to complete the following statement:

Ten possible characters (whether they are people I already have in mind for my story or people I would create) who could realistically have a strong reason to want my lead to achieve the story goal and be easily available to my lead are:

What would be this character's role in my story?	Why would this character want my lead to achieve the story goal?	Would this character be available to my lead? Where? When?
Example: Rosaline's assistant at the flower shop.	He has become fond of Rosaline since coming to work at the shop; also, the shop's survival is to his advantage, too.	Yes—every day at the shop, during work hours.
1.		
2.		
3.		
4.		

5.		
6.		
7.		
8.		
9.		
10.		

Now study your answers, imagining each possible confidant in action—involved in a warm, intimate and honest interaction with your lead—and answer the following questions:

Of all the above possibilities, the one I imagine would have the greatest potential
for true, honest intimacy with my lead is . . .   No. _____

Of all of the above possiblities, the one I find most interesting
as a character is . . .   No. _____

Of all the above possibilities, the one I think I would most
enjoy writing about is . . .   No. _____

Of all the above possibilities, the one I think I would provide the greatest
emotional support to my lead is . . .   No. _____

Confidant's Character Fact List

TRAIT	DESCRIPTION	WRITING COACH
Story Goal	To	◄ Must be to help lead achieve his or her story goal or simply to see him or her do so.
Gender		◄ Take from Confidant Worksheet, page 91.
Age		◄ A likely age, given the confidant's position and place in life, etc.
Physical		◄ Create a Confidant's Photo Collage on page 96.
Body Type		◄ Consult Confidant's Photo Collage. Thin? Svelte? Wiry? Fat? Husky? Stocky? Muscular? Scrawny? Voluptuous?
Height		◄ Consult Confidant's Photo Collage, Tall? Medium height? Short? Decide on an exact height.
Hair Color and Style		◄ Consult Confidant's Photo Collage. Blond, brown, black (raven), red, auburn, gray, white; light, medium, dark? Short, long, limp, teased, clean, dirty; a specific haircut?
Eye Color		◄ Consult Confidant's Photo Collage, Gray, green, blue, violet, brown, deep brown, hazel; a combination?
Mannerisms		◄ Study Confidant's Photo Collage and imagine this character in action. What is the most distinctive or noticeable mannerism?

Confidant's Character Fact List

TRAIT	DESCRIPTION	WRITING COACH
Distinctive Speech Pattern		◄ Study Confidant's Photo Collage and imagine this character speaking. What is the most distinctive feature of his/her way of speaking?
Personal		
Personality		◄ Draw clues from how you've defined your confidant so far, as well as from studying Confidant's Photo Collage.
Background		◄ Draw clues from how you've defined your opposition so far and from studying your Confidant's Photo Collage. Confidant's background needn't be as extensive as for lead.
Personal Life		◄ Your confidant's life when he or she isn't working. Draw clues from your confidant's life as you've defined it thus far. Consider kind of home, who else leves there, social life, leisure pursuits.

Confidant's Character Fact List

TRAIT	DESCRIPTION	WRITING COACH
Private Life		◀ Your confidant's life when he or she is alone. Draw clues from your confidant's life as you've defined it thus far. Consider hobbies and interests.
Work Life		◀ How your confidant earns his or her living. Draw clues from your confidant's life as you've defined it thus far. Include type of work, where he or she does it, the people he or she works with.
Strength		◀ Your confidant's strongest positive trait. Review above traits; which positive one stands out most visibly?
Weakness		◀ Your confidant's strongest negative trait. Review above traits; which negative one stands out most visibly?
Name		◀ Select a name that's appropriate for your confidant as you've defined him or her. See character naming advice on page 66. Enter name at bottom of Confidant's Photo Collage (page 96) and record it on Character Name Sheet (page 76).

Confidant's Photo Collage

Name:

CHAPTER 12

The Romantic Involvement

A fourth, though optional, major character to create before you start plotting your novel is the romantic involvement. Also known as the love interest or romantic interest, this character is the object of your lead's romantic interest. His or her story goal is to win the love of the lead, and this quest becomes one of your novel's subordinate story lines.

But not every novel needs this character. The decision whether to include a romantic involvement in your story depends on the kind of story you're telling.

Some Genres Require a Romantic Involvement

Does the genre of novel you're writing require a romantic involvement? You'll know the answer to this question from your reading in the genre. Needless to say, any sort of romance must contain a romantic involvement. Novels of romantic suspense require a character in this role, as do any novels in any genre whose name contains the word *romance* or *romantic*.

When Romance Is Optional

For other kinds of novels, the romantic involvement is optional. For example, some mysteries include a romantic involvement for the lead—the detective—and others do not. It's up to the author's preference, his instincts about what will work best in a given story. Thrillers, science fiction novels and horror novels are more examples of novels in which the romantic involvement is optional.

If a romantic involvement is optional for the kind of novel you're writing, consider the following questions in making the "to love" or "not to love" decision.

Would Your Lead's Present Circumstances Allow for a Romantic Involvement?

If you're writing a novel set in a maximum-security prison, a romantic involvement will be difficult for your lead. Is your lead already involved in a romantic relationship? Bear in mind that in a novel containing a romantic involvement, there is an evolving story line about this relationship between this character and your lead. If your lead is already married or in a committed romantic relationship, and you want to use the person she is already with as the romantic involvement, you must at the beginning of your story establish this relationship as unsatisfactory. For example, the lead may have an unhappy marriage or living-together relationship or be seeing someone he isn't in love with. Then as the story unfolds, show the two characters coming back together. Note also that in my novel writing plan, the lead and the romantic involvement always end up together, or at the very least there is an indication that they will.

Another option is to establish your lead in an unsatisfactory romantic relationship, then have her move toward a new person—the actual romantic involvement—as the story progresses. In the Marshall Plan the lead always ends up getting the guy or gal, so if you introduce a romantic involvement in a story where the lead is in an unsatisfactory relationship, the lead will have to end up having left the old partner for the romantic involvement.

What Effect Would a Romantic Relationship Have on the Evolution of the Story You're Planning?

As they do in real life, romance or the promise of romance, sex or the promise of sex, can add an interesting dimension, a texture and complexity, to a novel. Think about how a romantic or sexual attraction or involvement might impact your lead's pursuit of the story goal. Would it make this pursuit easier? More difficult? The best answer is the latter; anything that makes life harder for your lead is desirable in your novel.

The sometimes rocky development of a romance or sexual involvement can add not only tension to a novel, but also an element of conflict within the lead. One example of this dynamic would be a novel in which the lead is a high-powered lawyer who works grueling hours. His romantic involvement—let's say it's his new wife—resents the lead's almost constant absence. The lead is pulled in two directions: Should he continue to do what's necessary to succeed in his career, or accede to the demands of his lonely wife? Doubt, guilt, anxiety, tension, confusion, inner conflict—any and all of these possible by-products of romantic and/or sexual relationships make for more interesting reading in a novel.

Finally, consider that the lead's achievement of the story goal may be made infinitely more fulfilling, the world made even more "right" than before, if she has someone she loves with whom to share this achievement. Though you haven't yet plotted out your actual story, you'll probably be able to judge at this point whether this additional dimension would improve your story.

If, after having considered all of the previous factors, you feel a romantic involvement would not be right for the novel you're planning, turn to page 107. If you have decided to include this character in your novel, follow the guidelines below.

Creating the Romantic Involvement

The first step in casting the role of romantic involvement is to read back through your Story Idea and Lead's Character Fact List, searching for possible characters. If you don't find any likely candidates, consider whether a completely new character would be in order.

Perhaps, as with the opposition and confidant, you have already mentioned several possibilities, though not necessarily by name. If not, ponder now the sort of people with whom your lead would interact in the course of his daily routine.

Selecting the Most Effective Romantic Involvement for Your Lead

Most likely you'll light upon at least a few characters who could serve well as your lead's romantic involvement. Which one will work most effectively in your novel? The romantic involvement will be in close enough proximity to your lead often enough that a romantic relationship is possible and believable.

Use the Romantic Involvement Worksheet starting on page 101 to help with your brainstorming in order to arrive at the perfect choice.

Inevitably, at least one number will be repeated. This is the number of the character to use as your lead's romantic involvement.

The Romantic Involvement's Character Fact List

On the Romantic Involvement's Character Fact List starting on page 103, record your decisions about your lead's romantic involvement, whom you selected by using the Romantic Involvement Worksheet.

Your novel's romantic involvement is now a fully fleshed-out character, a person who will serve as a believable objective of romantic interest for your lead.

We're almost ready to begin plotting with the Blueprint. But first there's just one more step: designating as many of your novel's other, less important characters as you can at this stage. You'll find help with this in chapter thirteen.

Romantic Involvement Worksheet

Use the table below to complete the following statement:

Ten possible characters (whether they are people I already have in mind for my story or people I would create) who could serve as my lead's romantic involvement are:

What would be this character's role in my story?	Would my lead and this character have occasion to come together often and realistically?	Would a romantic/sexual relationship with this character add a dimension of tension or complexity to my story?
Example: Edward's young assistant professor at the University.	Yes—they meet often to review the curriculum and prepare lessons plans.	Yes—Edward is, or thinks he is, happily married to Bonnie.
1.		
2.		
3.		
4.		
5.		

6.		
7.		
8.		
9.		
10.		

Now review your answers, envisioning each possible romantic involvement in action—involved in moments of flirtation, attraction, perhaps lovemaking—with your lead. Then answer the following questions:

Of all the above possibilities, the one I imagine would have the greatest potential to both attract my lead and add tension, difficulty or complexity to his or her quest for the story goal is . . .   No. _____

Of all of the above possiblities, the one I find most interesting as a character is . . .   No. _____

Of all the above possibilities, the one I think I would most enjoy writing about is . . .   No. _____

Of all the above possibilities, the one I think my lead would end up happiest with is . . .   No. _____

Romantic Involvement's Character Fact List

TRAIT	DESCRIPTION	WRITING COACH
Story Goal	To	◀ Must be to win the love of the lead.
Gender		◀ Take from Romantic Involvement Sheet, page 101.
Age		◀ A likely age, given the romantic involvement's position and place in life, etc.
Physical		◀ Create a Romantic Involvement's Photo Collage on page 106.
Body Type		◀ Consult Romantic Involvement's Photo Collage. Thin? Svelte? Wiry? Fat? Husky? Stocky? Muscular? Scrawny? Voluptuous?
Height		◀ Consult Romantic Involvement's Photo Collage. Tall? Medium height? Short? Decide on an exact height.
Hair Color and Style		◀ Consult Romantic Involvement's Photo Collage. Blond, brown, black (raven), red, auburn, gray, white; light, medium, dark? Short, long, limp, teased, clean, dirty; a specific haircut?
Eye Color		◀ Consult Romantic Involvement's Photo Collage. Gray, green, blue, violet, brown, deep brown, hazel; a combination?
Mannerisms		◀ Study Romantic Involvement's Photo Collage and imagine this character in action. What is the most distinctive or noticeable mannerism?

Romantic Involvement's Character Fact List

TRAIT	DESCRIPTION	WRITING COACH
Distinctive Speech Pattern		◀ Study Romantic Involvement's Photo Collage and imagine this character speaking. What is the most distinctive feature of his/her way of speaking?
Personal		
Personality		◀ Draw clues from how you've defined your romantic involvement so far, as well as from studying Romantic Involvement's Photo Collage.
Background		◀ Draw clues from how you've defined your romantic involvement so far and from studying your Romantic Involvement's Photo Collage. Romantic involvement's background needn't be as extensive as for lead.
Personal Life		◀ Your romantic involvement's life when he or she isn't working. Draw clues from your romantic involvement's life as you've defined it thus far. Consider kind of home, who else leves there, social life, leisure pursuits.

Romantic Involvement's Character Fact List

TRAIT	DESCRIPTION	WRITING COACH
Private Life		◄ Your romantic ivolvement's life when he or she is alone. Draw clues from your romantic involvement's life as you've defined it thus far. Consider hobbies and interests.
Work Life		◄ How your romantic involvement earns his or her living. Draw clues from your romantic involvement's life as you've defined it thus far. Include type of work, where he or she does it, the people he or she works with.
Strength		◄ Your romantic involvement's strongest positive trait. Review above traits; which positive one stands out most visibly?
Weakness		◄ Your romantic involvement's strongest negative trait. Review above traits; which negative one stands out most visibly?
Name		◄ Select a name that's appropriate for your romantic involvement as you've defined him or her. See character naming advice on page 66. Enter name at bottom of Romantic Involvement Photo Collage (page 106) and record it on Character Name Sheet (page 76).

Romantic Involvement's Photo Collage

Name:_____

CHAPTER 13

Other Characters

Every novel contains numerous characters who play less important roles in the story than the lead, opposition, confidant and romantic involvement, yet are vital to the workings of the plot. Some of these characters may be nothing more than names from the past, but they may still be important.

At this stage you must formalize these characters. In doing so, you'll find that the world you've created for your lead thus far will come more sharply into focus—for it's often the details that define life, and fiction.

You'll be surprised to find that, whether or not you were aware of it, you've already created most of these lesser characters. Inevitably, you mentioned many of them in your character fact lists, though perhaps not by name. Maybe you wrote of "his assistant," "her doctor" or "his uncle." It's time now to bring these people more fully to life by naming them and including them in a Minor Characters List.

Reread all of your character fact lists, searching for such mentions. On the Minor Characters List on page 109, jot down the characters you've already named. If you come across a character you haven't yet named, jot down his function in the story (professor, cleaning man, etc.), and then take a moment to give this person a name. Refer to your Character Name Sheet (page 76) to see which letters of the alphabet are still unused, and use these letters now. See page 66 for character naming advice. If you run out of letters and must reuse one, make the names as different from each other as you can.

The characters you'll list now on your Minor Characters List are not necessarily *all* of your novel's characters; they're just the ones you're able to identify now. You will still be free to create characters as needed as you plot your story.

You have now created a complete virtual world for your lead, replete with a varied cast of characters. You have also presented your lead with a crisis that has in turn forced her to decide to go in search of the story goal, which will solve that crisis.

Armed with all of the above, you're ready now to start plotting.

Minor Characters List

NAME	FUNCTION
Example: Dr. Claudia Allen	Rhonda's Oncologist

PART IV

Plotting With the Blueprint

CHAPTER 14

Multiple Story Lines

In order to begin plotting your novel using the Blueprint, you must have an overall understanding of the concept of multiple story lines and how they work together.

Read the following principles carefully.

1. The number of story lines your novel will contain depends on your novel's length. The longer your novel, the more story lines you'll have.

2. Story lines belong to viewpoint characters only. A story line is plotted and written through the senses and awareness of a viewpoint character.

3. Every novel, regardless of its length, will have at its core two story lines: the lead's main story line (in which he or she pursues the story goal) and the lead's subplot. For this reason, you'll always have one more story line than you have viewpoint characters.

4. A novel at the shortest length range, 50,000–64,000 words, adds *one* additional story line—that of a second viewpoint character. This makes a total of three story lines: the lead's main story line, the lead's subplot and the second viewpoint character's story line.

    A novel at the longest length range, 140,000–154,000 words, adds *five* additional story lines—those of five more viewpoint characters. This makes a total of seven story lines: the lead's main story line, the lead's subplot and the story lines of each of the five additional viewpoint characters.

Who are these viewpoint characters?

The first viewpoint character is always your lead. The Marshall Plan Blueprint then designates other characters as viewpoint characters #1, #2 and so on, depending on the length of your novel, whether you're including a romantic involvement and whether your opposition is "visible" or not.

Use the following chart to determine how many viewpoint characters your novel should have. Then turn to the page indicated to determine your novel's story lines. You recorded your novel's target word length on page 25.

If your novel's word length will be . . .	Then your total number of viewpoint characters will be . . .
50,000–64,000 words	2 (below)
65,000–89,000 words	3 (go to page 113)
90,000—114,000 words	4 (go to page 114)
115,000–139,000 words	5 (go to page 115)
140,000–154,000 words	6 (go to page 116)

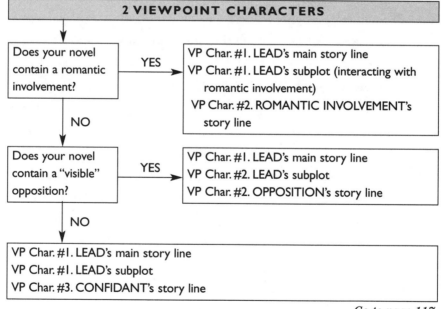

Go to page 117.

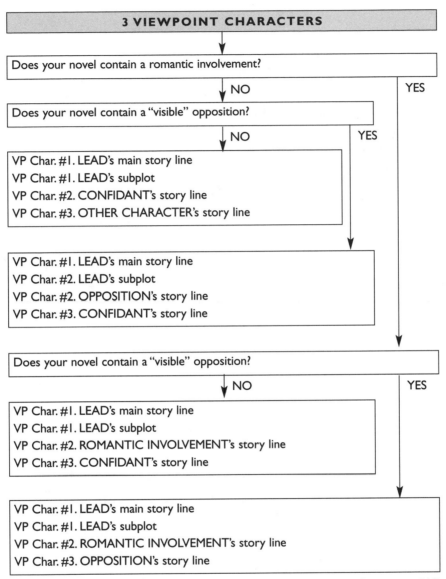

3 VIEWPOINT CHARACTERS

Does your novel contain a romantic involvement?

NO   YES

Does your novel contain a "visible" opposition?

NO   YES

VP Char. #1. LEAD's main story line
VP Char. #1. LEAD's subplot
VP Char. #2. CONFIDANT's story line
VP Char. #3. OTHER CHARACTER's story line

VP Char. #1. LEAD's main story line
VP Char. #2. LEAD's subplot
VP Char. #2. OPPOSITION's story line
VP Char. #3. CONFIDANT's story line

Does your novel contain a "visible" opposition?

NO   YES

VP Char. #1. LEAD's main story line
VP Char. #1. LEAD's subplot
VP Char. #2. ROMANTIC INVOLVEMENT's story line
VP Char. #3. CONFIDANT's story line

VP Char. #1. LEAD's main story line
VP Char. #1. LEAD's subplot
VP Char. #2. ROMANTIC INVOLVEMENT's story line
VP Char. #3. OPPOSITION's story line

Go to page 117.

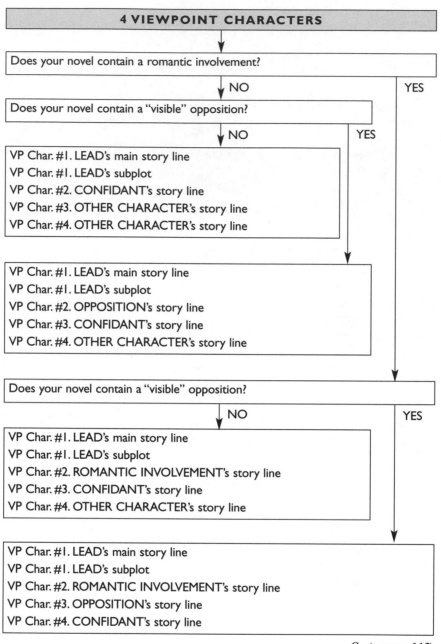

4 VIEWPOINT CHARACTERS

Does your novel contain a romantic involvement?

NO → / YES →

Does your novel contain a "visible" opposition?

NO → / YES →

VP Char. #1. LEAD's main story line
VP Char. #1. LEAD's subplot
VP Char. #2. CONFIDANT's story line
VP Char. #3. OTHER CHARACTER's story line
VP Char. #4. OTHER CHARACTER's story line

VP Char. #1. LEAD's main story line
VP Char. #1. LEAD's subplot
VP Char. #2. OPPOSITION's story line
VP Char. #3. CONFIDANT's story line
VP Char. #4. OTHER CHARACTER's story line

Does your novel contain a "visible" opposition?

NO → / YES →

VP Char. #1. LEAD's main story line
VP Char. #1. LEAD's subplot
VP Char. #2. ROMANTIC INVOLVEMENT's story line
VP Char. #3. CONFIDANT's story line
VP Char. #4. OTHER CHARACTER's story line

VP Char. #1. LEAD's main story line
VP Char. #1. LEAD's subplot
VP Char. #2. ROMANTIC INVOLVEMENT's story line
VP Char. #3. OPPOSITION's story line
VP Char. #4. CONFIDANT's story line

Go to page 117.

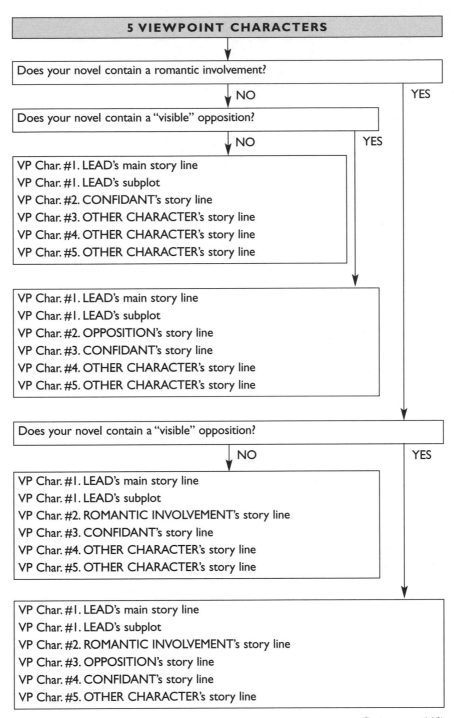

5 VIEWPOINT CHARACTERS

Does your novel contain a romantic involvement?

NO → YES

Does your novel contain a "visible" opposition?

NO → YES

VP Char. #1. LEAD's main story line
VP Char. #1. LEAD's subplot
VP Char. #2. CONFIDANT's story line
VP Char. #3. OTHER CHARACTER's story line
VP Char. #4. OTHER CHARACTER's story line
VP Char. #5. OTHER CHARACTER's story line

VP Char. #1. LEAD's main story line
VP Char. #1. LEAD's subplot
VP Char. #2. OPPOSITION's story line
VP Char. #3. CONFIDANT's story line
VP Char. #4. OTHER CHARACTER's story line
VP Char. #5. OTHER CHARACTER's story line

Does your novel contain a "visible" opposition?

NO → YES

VP Char. #1. LEAD's main story line
VP Char. #1. LEAD's subplot
VP Char. #2. ROMANTIC INVOLVEMENT's story line
VP Char. #3. CONFIDANT's story line
VP Char. #4. OTHER CHARACTER's story line
VP Char. #5. OTHER CHARACTER's story line

VP Char. #1. LEAD's main story line
VP Char. #1. LEAD's subplot
VP Char. #2. ROMANTIC INVOLVEMENT's story line
VP Char. #3. OPPOSITION's story line
VP Char. #4. CONFIDANT's story line
VP Char. #5. OTHER CHARACTER's story line

Go to page 117.

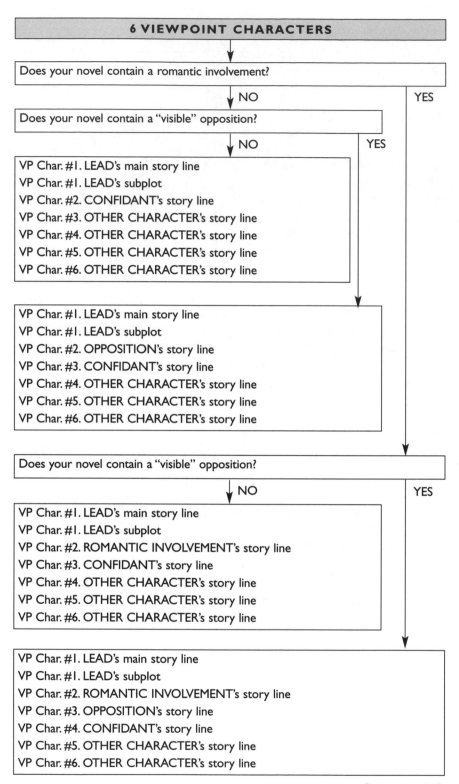

6 VIEWPOINT CHARACTERS

Does your novel contain a romantic involvement?

↓ NO   YES

Does your novel contain a "visible" opposition?

↓ NO   YES

VP Char. #1. LEAD's main story line
VP Char. #1. LEAD's subplot
VP Char. #2. CONFIDANT's story line
VP Char. #3. OTHER CHARACTER's story line
VP Char. #4. OTHER CHARACTER's story line
VP Char. #5. OTHER CHARACTER's story line
VP Char. #6. OTHER CHARACTER's story line

VP Char. #1. LEAD's main story line
VP Char. #1. LEAD's subplot
VP Char. #2. OPPOSITION's story line
VP Char. #3. CONFIDANT's story line
VP Char. #4. OTHER CHARACTER's story line
VP Char. #5. OTHER CHARACTER's story line
VP Char. #6. OTHER CHARACTER's story line

Does your novel contain a "visible" opposition?

↓ NO   YES

VP Char. #1. LEAD's main story line
VP Char. #1. LEAD's subplot
VP Char. #2. ROMANTIC INVOLVEMENT's story line
VP Char. #3. CONFIDANT's story line
VP Char. #4. OTHER CHARACTER's story line
VP Char. #5. OTHER CHARACTER's story line
VP Char. #6. OTHER CHARACTER's story line

VP Char. #1. LEAD's main story line
VP Char. #1. LEAD's subplot
VP Char. #2. ROMANTIC INVOLVEMENT's story line
VP Char. #3. OPPOSITION's story line
VP Char. #4. CONFIDANT's story line
VP Char. #5. OTHER CHARACTER's story line
VP Char. #6. OTHER CHARACTER's story line

Go to page 117.

Other Characters' Story Lines

If the flow chart indicates that your novel will require "OTHER CHAR-ACTER's story lines," you'll have to select these characters from your Minor Characters List starting on page 109. Which ones should you choose? Ask yourself the following questions in deciding:

- After my lead, opposition, romantic involvement (if any) and confidant, which of these characters could conceivably play the next most important role(s) in my story as I see it so far?
- Which of these characters might have strong reason to either support or oppose my lead in his pursuit of the story goal?
- Which of these characters could conceivably have story goals of their own?
- From which of these characters' viewpoints would I enjoy writing?

Consider these questions as you select your other viewpoint characters. They must play important roles in the story, be firmly for or against your lead, have story lines (goals) of their own and be interesting to write about.

Once you've selected as many of these other characters as you need, use this decision, along with the results of the previous flowcharts, to complete the form on page 119 for easy reference. (See the following page for an example.)

CHARACTER	NAME	VP CHAR. #
LEAD	Jim Tanner	1
ROMANTIC INVOLVEMENT (if any)	Laura Gomez	2
OPPOSITION (if "visible")		
CONFIDANT	Allen Feinstein	3
OTHER CHARACTER	Karla Hunt	4
OTHER CHARACTER	Barbee Chin	5
OTHER CHARACTER	Stu Johnson	6
OTHER CHARACTER		

CHART	NAME	VP CHAR. #
LEAD		1
ROMANTIC INVOLVEMENT (if any)		
OPPOSITION (if "visible)		
CONFIDANT		
OTHER CHARACTER		
OTHER CHARACTER		
OTHER CHARACTER		
OTHER CHARACTER		

You have now created all of your principle characters and established which ones will take center stage by serving as viewpoint characters, the characters whose senses and awareness you will tell your story through. How will you move them through the novel?

Subplots and Story Lines

Your lead will have two story lines: the lead's main story line and the lead's subplot. Your novel may also contain story lines presented through the viewpoint of the romantic involvement, the opposition, the confidant and up to four other characters.

With any of your viewpoint characters, you'll begin with an overall story goal: possession of or relief from something, just as with the lead's main story line, though this goal needn't arise from a crisis. Only the lead's main story line must arise from a crisis. Once you have decided on a character's story line—what she will pursue—have the character set smaller, one-at-a-time goals intended to take that character nearer and nearer to achieving the story goal. We'll go into finer detail about this goal-seeking pattern in the next chapter; for now, speaking more generally, it's enough to say that each time the character tries to achieve one of these smaller goals, engaging in a confrontation, argument, search, evasion and so on—she fails. (The only exception to this rule is the opposition, who ends each of her efforts in success.) After each of these small failures, the lead sets a new minigoal that she believes *will* take her nearer to the story goal.

Problems, obstacles, fights, evasions and struggles all make for the conflict that constitutes good storytelling. Readers (and movie viewers, for that matter) love to root for a lead in trouble and love to worry that the lead won't ever achieve the story goal. That's why it was so important for you to make your lead sympathetic by endowing him with likability, competence, virtue and courage. A reader won't root for someone she doesn't care about.

It's because a lead meeting failure after failure is so important to storytelling—in fact, constitutes the very essence of plotting—that your opposition, unlike all your other characters, will succeed in achieving each of his minigoals. Either the opposition has a goal that's in direct conflict with that of the lead, or his goal is to stop the lead from achieving her story goal. The opposition's smaller goals will, therefore, be toward this end. Each time the opposition succeeds, the lead's situation grows worse. *Bad* situation for your lead = *good* storytelling.

Let's discuss briefly how each of the specific story lines in your novel should evolve.

The Lead's Main Story Line

The lead's main story line is the one in which he pursues the story goal, which he or she believes will solve the crisis. It's the story line you created as part of your story idea.

The Lead's Subplot

The lead's subplot carries your lead in pursuit of a lesser goal than the story goal. This lesser goal may or may not be related to the story goal. Of course, over the course of your novel, your lead will undoubtedly pursue lots of smaller goals. The lead's subplot, however, is a formalization of this concept and runs through the entire novel.

Why include a lead's subplot? First, it adds interest and texture to your novel. A novel in which the lead is constantly focused on achieving the main story goal, without ever thinking of anything else, can make for tedious reading. The lead's subplot gives the lead and your readers the occasional break from the story's main action, at the same time adding another layer of drama to your tale.

A story in which the lead pursues several goals at once is also more realistic. In real life, we do not pursue even our most urgent goals in a vacuum. Issues involving our families, jobs and friends often weave— or barge—their way into what we're trying to get done, distracting us.

This kind of distraction can also add tension to your novel. The reader may worry that the secondary goal the lead is pursuing may prevent her from achieving the main story goal. In a novel, tension is good. It keeps readers reading. It's what keeps readers "on the edge of their seats," unable "to put your book down."

When you devise your lead's subplot, have him pursue possession of or relief from something, as with the lead's main story line; however, this goal needn't be in response to a crisis.

If your novel will have a romantic involvement, the lead's subplot will be about the lead's evolving relationship with this character. As you develop this relationship in your story, bear in mind two elements that make for maximum drama and effectiveness in any romantic story line—internal conflict and external conflict.

Internal Conflict

Internal conflict is what it sounds like: an inner, or emotional, resistance within a character that makes her reluctant or unwilling to enter into a committed romantic relationship.

For example, a woman who finds herself drawn to a man who is a recovered alcoholic, but who remembers her father abusing her mother in his drunken rages, might experience inner conflict with respect to committing to this man. It is *inside* factors that keep the two apart.

Because it's the lead who will be hesitant to enter into a relationship with the romantic involvement, the lead should always have an inner conflict about committing to this character. However, even though the romantic involvement's story goal is to win the lead's love, this character can still have an inner conflict of her own. This will only make the story more interesting and layered.

Study your Lead's Character Fact List for possible clues to an inner conflict for your lead. Most likely you'll find the best possibilities in the background section. If you don't, it's perfectly legitimate to add something to the lead's background now that would create an inner conflict downstream.

External Conflict

A romantic story thread should also have an external conflict between the two characters, keeping them from immediately getting together. An external conflict is an external, situational factor that becomes an obstacle to a committed relationship.

For example, a man who is an attorney and, through a series of freak circumstances, falls in love with the woman his client is suing, will suffer an external conflict (not to mention a conflict of interest) about this relationship. It is *outside* factors that keep the two apart.

Since it's your lead who will resist the romantic involvement's advances, it's your lead who must perceive an external conflict with respect to this relationship. However, as with the inner conflict, the romantic involvement can perceive this external conflict as well, even as he tries to win the lead's love. A more textured and interesting story is the result.

Review the character fact lists for both your lead and your romantic involvement, looking for situational elements that could keep these two romantically apart. It's perfectly acceptable to add these elements to the character fact lists now if you have to.

The Romantic Involvement's Story Line

If your novel includes a romantic involvement, the romantic thread it creates in your story is the lead's subplot.

If your novel will contain a romantic involvement, and you thought this character and your lead would immediately come together in romantic harmony, you couldn't have been more wrong! In the Marshall Plan, the romantic involvement's story goal is, quite simply, to win the lead's love. When you create those passages of your novel that will be from the romantic involvement's viewpoint, his minigoals will always involve winning over the lead romantically.

Your lead will generally seek to resist the romantic involvement's advances, though he or she may falter occasionally in this resistance. This push-pull is what makes a novel's romantic thread interesting . . . and realistic.

Here, then, is how the dynamic between your lead and your romantic involvement works. When you're creating an encounter between these two characters, *and the encounter is from the lead's viewpoint*, the lead will seek to achieve minigoals with respect to her subplot—resisting the romantic involvement's advances. But since the lead always fails to achieve these minigoals, these encounters must end with a failure to resist. In other words, the lead succumbs, weakens or in some other way fails to repel the romantic involvement. When you're creating an encounter between these two characters, *and the encounter is from the romantic involvement's viewpoint*, the romantic involvement will seek to achieve minigoals with respect to her story line—winning the lead's love. But since the romantic involvement, like all other characters except the opposition, always fails to achieve these minigoals, these encounters must end with the romantic involvement's failure to win the lead's love; in other words, in these encounters the lead successfully resists. An encounter's outcome all depends on the viewpoint through which you're telling the story.

The Opposition's Story Line

The opposition's story goal is to achieve something that will make it impossible for the lead to achieve his story goal or simply to stop the lead from achieving his story goal. The opposition is the only character whose encounters in pursuit of those minigoals end in success. This means encounters between your lead and your opposition, regardless of whose viewpoint you're in, end the same way. Lead's viewpoint: Lead fails. Opposition's viewpoint: Opposition succeeds. Same result.

The Confidant's Story Line

The goal of the confidant is to see the lead achieve *her* goal. Think of the confidant as a booster, a supporter, moral support. When you create passages of your novel from your confidant's viewpoint, however, the confidant, like all other characters except the opposition, will fail in achieving his smaller goals. For example, you might create an encounter, from your confidant's viewpoint, in which the confidant is trying to convince the lead to do something the confidant believes will help the lead achieve her story goal. The confidant would fail to convince the lead, and this outcome would create more doubt in the mind of the reader—more of the tension we seek to create in the novel.

The confidant might also engage in an encounter with some other character, again in an attempt to attain a small goal that will bring the lead closer to achieving her story goal. Here, too, the confidant would fail.

What if the confidant was in an encounter with the opposition? It would end up very much like an encounter between the opposition and the lead herself. If you create the passage from the confidant's viewpoint, the confidant fails. If you create the passage from the opposition's viewpoint, the opposition—as always—succeeds. The net result is the same.

Other Characters' Story Lines

The other characters you may have needed as viewpoint characters will each have their own story goals. They, too, will fail to achieve their minigoals. If they engage in encounters with the opposition, the opposition succeeds.

These other characters won't be on stage much, so their story goals should be smaller. They should also be related to the lead's story goal in some way. Think of these other characters as the little fish who swim alongside the big fish. Some of them help the big fish by keeping it clean; others are an annoyance, nipping at its sides. Either way, they're carried along on the big fish's route—small pieces of the big picture.

Rotating Story Lines

In chapter seventeen, where you'll actually plot with the Blueprint, you'll find that the Blueprint takes much of the guesswork out of plotting, leading you through many of your storytelling decisions. Sometimes the Blueprint will tell you whose viewpoint to use at a particular time, but very often it won't. At these times it's up to you to juggle your various story lines.

Following are some general tips on story-line juggling.

Develop a Rough Hierarchy

In my book *The Marshall Plan for Novel Writing*, I included a table called the NovelMaster that stated exactly how much story space to give each viewpoint character. The actual data in the table isn't as important as the general message behind it: Your lead must be given more space than any other character. It is, after all, the lead's story you're telling. Readers will not only want to spend most of their reading time with this character, they won't want to be away from him for too long. (See Keep All the Balls in the Air, below.)

Similarly, a less important character, lower on the hierarchy (for example, your viewpoint character #5 is less important than your viewpoint character #2) should be given less space than the lead. The least important viewpoint character would be given the least space of all.

Keep All the Balls in the Air

Don't leave any one story line for too long if you can help it. Of course, in the case of the least important viewpoint characters, who won't be allotted much space, you'll have to go awhile between their appearances. Otherwise, do your best to rotate your story lines so the reader can keep tabs on everyone. A danger of waiting too long before returning to a character is that the reader will have forgotten where that character left off—or won't care!

Don't Forget That Life Goes On

Depending on the structure of your story, you'll sometimes leave a character at a certain time and place, and return to that character exactly when and where you left him. At other times you'll leave a character at one time and place, and return to that character at a later time, somewhere else. In the latter case, life for this character didn't just stand still; she will have been living her life and going about her every-day business in the meantime, which will naturally have an effect on her situation and behavior now.

When you're plotting and writing, keep this useful fact in mind. While the character was offstage, he could have done things that are necessary in his daily life or even necessary to your plot, but that are not especially interesting or pertinent to the story you're telling. If something happened to the character that *was* relevant to the story, he can talk about it, or if you're in this character's viewpoint, you can have him think about it.

Keep Your Viewpoints Straight

There will be times as you write your novel when you'll have encounters between two viewpoint characters. At these times it's important to be clear in your mind as to whose encounter this is. In other words, which of these viewpoint characters is the viewpoint character for *this* encounter? It makes a big difference. The reader can only know what the viewpoint character thinks and is aware of. For this reason, the same encounter from two different viewpoints would read quite differently.

Keep Your Lead's Two Story Lines Separate

To avoid confusion for both yourself and your readers, keep your lead's main story line separate from her subplot. In other words, when you're writing about your lead, have her pursuing one goal or the other, but not both. Of course, it wouldn't be realistic to pretend that when she is pursuing one goal, the other doesn't exist. Just make sure that when we're with your lead, she is working toward only one of her goals at a time. The lead's main story line is by far the more important of his threads; therefore, devote more space to it than to the lead's subplot.

Almost There . . .

By this time you're no doubt itching to get plotting. That's coming up. But first I have two more things to tell you about: section sheets (the building blocks of plotting), and story surprises. These are the subjects of the next two chapters.

CHAPTER 15

Section Sheets

In the Marshall Plan, the building blocks of a plot are sections, individual units of story action. The tool for planning each of these sections is a template called the section sheet.

Nowhere in this book or in *The Marshall Plan for Novel Writing* will you find the word *scene*. That's because the Marshall Plan does not use the scene concept. This is an important point; understanding it will save you a lot of confusion. My plotting system uses sections.

There are two types of sections: the action section and the reaction section. There are therefore two types of section sheets: the action section sheet and the reaction section sheet.

When should you use an action section, and when should you use a reaction section?

Most of the sections in your novel will be action sections. In an action section, a viewpoint character pursues one of the small goals that she believes will bring her closer to achieving her story goal. In most cases, at the end of the action section the character will set a new short-term goal and move directly into pursuing it in the next action section.

Occasionally, however, when it's appropriate to show a character reacting to an especially devastating failure (or to show the opposition reacting to an especially satisfying success) or when you must show a character in the process of analyzing what has just happened and setting a new short-term goal, a reaction section is in order.

The Action Section in Depth

Let's begin with an overview of what happens in an action section. A viewpoint character, reacting to what happened in his previous section, now pursues a new short-term goal intended to help him attain the story goal. The section customarily includes another character who is the primary other "player" in the section. (There may be other people present, though they will not play the functional role that the primary other character will.) Sometimes no other character is present, as in the case of the viewpoint character looking for or running from someone or something.

Whether or not anyone else is present, the viewpoint character tries to achieve the short-term goal, engages in conflict and ultimately fails to achieve her short-term goal. The exception to this rule is the opposition, who succeeds.

At the end of an action section, you have two choices: to move directly into a new action section or use a reaction section. If the failure has been especially devastating or if extensive analysis is called for, you would go next to a reaction section. Otherwise you would go to a new action section. Either way, what has occurred in the section that has just taken place drives the events of this character's new section.

On page 135 you'll find a sample action section sheet. Its components are keyed to the detailed instructions that follow.

❶ *Section Character*

Enter the name of this section's viewpoint character. Review the guidelines for story line juggling starting on page 125 for tips on switching back and forth among your viewpoint characters.

❷ *Where*

Describe where this section will take place. What would be a logical setting for this section, in light of the character your viewpoint character will be confronting, or what he hopes to accomplish? Sometimes it's useful to consult the Character Fact List for a section's viewpoint character, to remind yourself of where she lives, works and plays, and of places she routinely goes.

When you're deciding where to set a section, keep the following points in mind.

Unexpected Locations Make for More Interesting Reading

Can you think of a reason why your viewpoint character might confront this other character, seek something or someone, or seek to evade something or someone in a place the reader would not normally think of these things happening? Remember Orson Welles and Rita Hayworth's final confrontation in the hall of mirrors at the climax of the movie *The Lady*

From Shanghai? Most people who have seen this film recall the ending vividly because of its unexpected fun house/mirror maze setting. This kind of juxtaposition of disparate elements, when not overused, can be extremely effective.

The Fewer People in a Section Aside From Your Viewpoint Character and the Character He or She Is Opposing, the Better

To be more exact, the fewer *speaking* people, the better. A section is at its most powerful when it focuses on two people confronting each other without extraneous distractions. Setting a section at a party or in a restaurant, with people around but not speaking, still qualifies as leaving your two opponents alone. The surrounding people, in these cases, are more in the nature of props or stage-setting than people.

A *Where* Needn't Necessarily Be Stationary

Novels are not plays, in which each act must take place in one location. On paper, anything's possible, and features that would be impossible in a play or expensive in a movie cost nothing in a novel. A *where*, then, could be a sprawling ranch on which the lead and the romantic involvement ride on horseback, the inside of a car involved in a riveting chase or the sidewalk where two characters simply walk and talk. In other words, a *where* can move.

❸ *When*

State when this section is taking place. This feature is most useful when you express the time of the section not only in absolute time, but also relative to this viewpoint character's last section. For example: Monday, 4:00 P.M.—the next day.

Keep the following points in mind as you plan your novel's time frame.

The Tighter the Better

Keep the action of your novel restricted to the smallest amount of time possible. Your story will have more immediacy and move more quickly.

Allow for Intervening Events

Tracking time correctly in a novel is vital. When you decide when a section will take place, take into account anything this character—or the character he is now confronting—would have had to do offstage beforehand. Allow also for events to occur that one or both of these characters must now know about. Finally, be realistic in terms of travel time. Don't create a section about a character in California on Friday morning, and follow it with a section about that character in Boston that day for lunch. It's just not physically possible—at least, not yet.

A good copyeditor is invaluable for, among many things, making sure time tracks correctly in a novel. But proper time tracking is first the novelist's responsibility, a sign of professionalism and attention to detail. Moreover, if your timing is severely off, even the most proficient copyeditor won't be able to untangle it, and when you try to do so, your story may collapse like a house of cards.

If necessary, keep a separate list of when your sections take place, including their locations when relevant. If it's helpful, you can also draw links between a character's sections for easier tracking. Consider a simple format like the following:

Viewpoint Character	*Time*
Gretchen	Friday, August 23, noon
	(The Plaza, New York City)
Harrison	Friday, August 23, 7:00 P.M.
Gretchen	Saturday, August 24, late evening
	(Norwalk, CT)
Kyle	Saturday, August 24, 11:00 P.M.

Try Not to Spin Your Wheels or Back Up

Sometimes we read a novel in which an event is shown from one character's viewpoint, then the author moves backward in time to show the same event from another participating character's viewpoint. Or we read of one character's actions during a certain period of time, then move backward to learn what another character was doing at the same time.

Try to avoid using both of these techniques unless they're absolutely necessary. Editors don't like them, and neither do most readers. The reason is that both techniques stop the story and make it go backwards, as it were. The reader must then read through the same "time" again to get back to where she was. Any device that slows, stops or "reruns" your story is undesirable. Flashbacks are disliked by many editors and readers for this reason (see page 230).

❹ *Goal From Character's Last Section*

State here what short-term goal this character set at the end of his last section sheet. Examples: "To convince Phyllis to give him the letter." "To find a piece of evidence that proves Howard was in the house." "To escape Andrew."

By stating the goal here, you leave no room for doubt about what the viewpoint character hopes to accomplish in this section. It's also a good reminder for you as you plan the action of the section itself. Finally, you may use it later as you write out the section in actual fiction prose.

❺ *Against*

Enter the name of the character whom this section's viewpoint character will confront in this section. If no other character will be present (as in the case of a search or escape, for instance), simply leave this line blank.

❻ *Conflict*

This section represents the heart—and major portion—of the section. The conflict it describes is the essence of the section, just as conflict is the essence of your novel as a whole. Just as readers want to worry in general about whether your lead will achieve her story goal, when reading about various characters' individual encounters they want to worry about whether the characters will achieve their short-term goals.

If you have an opposing character in the section, that character must have a strong reason for wanting the viewpoint character not to achieve the short-term goal. Or, the opposing character must be in pursuit of a short-term goal of his own, the achievement of which will prevent the viewpoint character's success.

The opposing character needn't always be the opposition. The opposing character may be any other character, viewpoint or not, who would have reason to oppose the viewpoint character in her pursuit.

Keep in mind also that as many sections as possible should have opposing characters, rather than being sections in which the viewpoint character acts alone (chases, searches, etc.). Readers want as much actual person-against-person conflict as they can get, and our job is to give readers what they want.

Whoever your opposing character is, her behavior in this section will be driven by a desire to oppose the viewpoint character. Describe in summary form the main points of this encounter. Whether it's an argument, a discussion, a calm conversation or a physical fight, write down the main "parries" and "thrusts" of the conflict in whatever form it takes—chasing, arguing, cajoling, fleeing, talking, waiting, fighting, seducing, insisting, demanding searching, wheedling, manipulating. . . .

A mistake many beginning novelists make is to fail to wring enough conflict out of this encounter. The viewpoint character tries one tack, perhaps another, then gives up. Be sure to milk the confrontation for all it's worth. When you're unsure or in doubt about whether you've done this, see if your viewpoint character has tried at least three distinct tacks in her effort to attain the section goal. If there aren't three, you've stopped the conflict too soon.

❼ *Failure (Unless Opposition)*

This is where you describe the form failure takes for this section's viewpoint character—unless the viewpoint character is the opposition, in which case you describe his success.

A failure may take any of three forms:

1. The viewpoint character simply fails to achieve the section goal.

2. The viewpoint character not only fails to achieve the section goal, but she also learns of a new, even larger problem or obstacle that makes the general situation (with respect to reaching the story goal) even worse.

3. The viewpoint character does achieve the section goal but at the same time learns of a new, even larger problem or obstacle than the one he has just overcome. This problem or obstacle makes the general situation (with respect to reaching the story goal) even worse.

Keep the following three points in mind as you devise your failures.

The Failure Must Be Logical

The failure, whatever form it takes, must be a logical outcome of the conflict that has just transpired. In other words, the failure cannot be a setback or revelation out of the blue, having nothing to do with the struggle that just took place. Let's say you have your viewpoint character, the romantic involvement, in the park, trying to convince your lead to go out with her tonight. Failure for the romantic involvement might be the lead's simply saying no and walking away (failure type 1). Or it might be the lead saying no *and* revealing that he already has a steady girlfriend (failure type 2). Or it might be the lead agreeing to go out with her tonight, but then adding that he'd better make it clear, in case the romantic involvement has any ideas, that because of certain events in his past the lead could never become seriously involved with anyone (failure type 3). The failure could *not* be the romantic involvement's suddenly getting hit on the head by a baseball.

Never Employ Coincidence

Coincidence, though common in real life, is a no-no in novels. Readers find it contrived—because it is! For this reason, never have the failure involve chance or coincidence. An example of a failure involving coincidence would be a character cursing someone out on the subway for rudeness, then arriving at a job interview to discover that the person's he's got the interview with is the person he cursed out.

Hit the Viewpoint Character Hard

A failure that comes slowly, or in bits and pieces, loses most if not all of its dramatic impact. When you introduce a failure, bring it down hard—swiftly and suddenly—to get the most out of it. Think of it as the curtain at the end of act two in a play: In a crisp instant we see that the situation has turned very dark for this character.

❽ *New Goal (or Go To a Reaction Section)*

Here you have two choices:

1. Have the viewpoint character devise a new short-term, section goal as a result of the failure she has just experienced, so that she is ready for another action section; or

2. Go to a reaction section.

Let's discuss each possibility.

New Goal

Most of the time you'll have your viewpoint character devise a new goal at the end of an action section, setting himself up for another action section. Note: When you write this section, you won't necessarily *show* the viewpoint character devising this new goal and then stating it. Most of the time it's unnecessary to do this, since the character will probably state his new goal in the next section, or his behavior will make this goal implicit. Stating the new goal here is for your own plotting purposes.

For example, in an action section, your viewpoint character has been trying to convince her boss not to fire her. The failure comes when the boss states flatly that her decision is final. Your viewpoint character's new short-term goal as a result of this failure is to appeal to her boss's boss. However, when you write out this section, you needn't necessarily have your viewpoint character state this goal, because in the next moment (the next action section) she stomps into her boss's boss's office and starts appealing to *him*. To have her state her new goal and then immediately act on it would be unnatural and redundant.

Go to a Reaction Section

Sometimes a viewpoint character's emotional reaction to a failure is such that you need story space to describe it; it would seem strange if you didn't. If the failure was especially devastating, most likely the character will respond strongly and will have to carefully weigh her present options. Or if the failure necessitates an especially large amount of ruminating or analyzing at this stage—as in a detective novel, for example—you'll need story space to show this. As a general rule, the more serious or meaningful the failure, the likelier it is you'll want to go to a reaction section.

If you do decide to go to a reaction section, simply write "TO REACTION SECTION" in this space. And, of course, when you next present this character, whether immediately following or a number of sections down the line, do so in a reaction section. We'll discuss the reaction section next.

Action

Section Character: ❶

Where: ❷

When: ❸

Goal From Character's Last Section	❹
Against	❺
Conflict	❻
Failure (Unless Opposition)	❼
New Goal (OR Go to a Reaction Section)	❽

The Reaction Section in Depth

In your novel you won't use a lot of reaction sections, relatively speaking. There's no hard and fast rule about how many to use. The more emotional and dramatic your story, the more you'll probably need.

On page 139 you'll find a blank reaction section sheet. Its components are keyed to the following detailed instructions.

❶ *Section Character*

Enter the name of the viewpoint character this reaction section is about. A reaction section doesn't have to immediately follow the action section it is paired with. You might put one or more other characters' sections in between.

❷ *Where*

Sometimes a reaction section is an immediate follow-up to an action section, the viewpoint character not even moving. Of course, in this case the *where* would be the same as that of this character's preceding action section. Other times your viewpoint character may be reacting in a different place. If so, tell us where he is.

❸ *When*

If this reaction section immediately follows this viewpoint character's action section, then this *when* may be only a few minutes later. Sometimes, though, a character reacts to failures later (usually somewhere else). Whatever the case, enter here the time at which this section takes place.

❹ *Failure From Character's Last Action Section*

Here you must briefly restate the failure this viewpoint character is responding to. This is not only for your own plotting purposes; you must also convey to the reader what this failure means to the character. For example: "Toby has sneaked Robert's designs to Ultra Interiors. They're sure to copy them. Robert will certainly lose his job—and his own company may very well sue him."

❺ *With*

Will this character be with another character during this reaction section? Very often that other character is the confidant, though it could be anyone. Consider the circumstances and whether anyone else would likely be present. If you decide to include another character, enter her name here. You'll convey your viewpoint character's reaction to the failure primarily through his dialogue with this character. If your viewpoint character will be alone, in which case you'll have to convey his reaction through thoughts and actions, leave this line blank.

❻ *Emotional*

This phase and the one that follows, Rational, constitute the largest portion of the reaction section. The reaction section is not about conflict, as the action section is; it's about reacting to adversity. Even when another character is present, there shouldn't be fighting between them; more likely there will be sympathizing, the giving of moral support and the trying out of ideas on how to proceed.

It's human nature to react to adversity according to a basic pattern. First we react emotionally, with our heart rather than our head. Here's where you describe the feelings your viewpoint character experiences as a result of the failure she has just experienced. A character might be furious, enraged, incensed, insulted, afraid, disappointed, heartbroken, embarrassed, frustrated, demoralized, disillusioned—whatever emotion would be natural under the circumstances.

If your character is with someone else, you'll have him express these feelings through conversation. If your character is alone, you'll convey the feelings through his thoughts and perhaps actions.

❼ *Rational*

Once the feelings have passed, the viewpoint character calms down, at least somewhat, pulls herself together and reacts with her head—rationally, without emotion clouding her judgment.

It's in this phase of the reaction section that you show your viewpoint character analyzing the failure, trying to grasp exactly what has happened. A detective in a mystery would work to interpret clues at this point.

Next comes a consideration of the various courses of action open to your character—the weighing of options with respect to the next short-term goal. The ramifications of each possible course are considered; some possibilities are rejected. It's important, of course, for these various possibilities to be logical options for the character to think of in light of the situation and the character's life. Review your Lead's Character Fact List (page 70) for ideas, if necessary.

❽ *New Goal*

In the reaction section you *do* show your viewpoint character finally deciding on what he feels is the best next course of action. State that here. This course of action, this pursuit of a new short-term goal, will be the subject of this character's next section, an action section.

Beads on a String

You should now have a clear grasp of how sections interconnect to form a story. Just to recap the basics:

1. Use an action section to show a viewpoint character in pursuit of a short-term goal that she believes will bring her nearer to achieving the story goal.

2. In most cases, follow an action section with another action section.

3. If a failure is especially severe, and extended reacting or analyzing is called for, show the character's reaction to the failure in an action section.

4. A reaction section always comes after an action section for the character being shown.

5. Never use two reaction sections in a row.

Reaction

Section Character: ❶

Where: ❷

When: ❸

❹ Failure from Character's Last Action Section

❺ With

❻ Emotional

❼ Rational

❽ New Goal

CHAPTER 16

Shaping a Plot

In the last chapter you learned how to build a plot on the micro level. Let's pull back now for a look at a well-plotted novel's broader lines—some points to keep in mind as you use the Blueprint in the following chapter.

Overall Structure

My plotting system uses the classic Aristotelian three-part story structure: beginning, middle and end. When using the Marshall Plan Blueprint, it's important to keep this structure in mind.

- The beginning of a novel is roughly the first quarter of the book. Thus the beginning of a four hundred-page novel would be about the first one hundred pages.
- The middle of a novel comes next and comprises approximately half the novel's length. The middle of a four hundred-page novel would be roughly pages one hundred to three hundred.
- The end of a novel is roughly its last quarter. Thus the last quarter of a four hundred-page novel is its last one hundred pages.

Classic Aristotelian Story Structure

BEGINNING	MIDDLE	END

Let's take each segment in turn and discuss points you should keep in mind as you work on each of them.

The Beginning

• The beginning of the novel is where you establish all of the important elements of your story—the setup. Your lead is introduced living his normal life when the crisis hits, causing him to set a goal that, when achieved, he believes will restore life to normal.

• Introduce all of your viewpoint characters in the beginning, making sure each has at least one viewpoint section of his own.

• Other characters who will be present through some or much of your story should also be introduced in the beginning. Either include them in viewpoint characters' sections, or at least have characters mention or think about them.

• Present all of your background in your novel's beginning. (See page 231.)

• The last section of the beginning is an action section called surprise #1. (Story surprises are discussed separately starting on page 144.)

The Middle

• You must work hard to make sure the middle, your novel's longest segment, is interesting to read and does not sag or drag.

• As the middle progresses, gradually worsen your lead's failures. Raise the stakes for your lead, raising the tension for your readers.

• Don't be afraid to take your lead on tangents as part of her pursuit of the story goal. Sometimes before you can do one thing, you must do something else, and before you can do the something else, you must do something else . . . and so on. This is perfectly legitimate plotting and is used frequently by veteran novelists. It's the way life often works, and it's an effective way to both complicate and create story for your book's middle.

• In the middle of the middle—the midpoint of your novel—you'll create an action section called surprise #2. At the end of your novel's middle, or three-quarters of the way through your book, you'll create an action section called surprise #3.

The End

• The end is the wrap-up, the segment in which all of your story elements come together.

• As the end progresses, give your lead fewer choices in terms of possible short-term goals; limit his options, thereby increasing the general sense of urgency. Here are four methods for doing this.

Use Your Opposition

Your opposition may very well have created some dead ends for your lead earlier in your novel. Here in your book's end, the opposition should certainly do so. Create some opportunities for your lead—some short-term goals for her to chase—and then have the opposition destroy them.

Eliminate Possible Courses of Action

This technique is similar to the previous one, except that the dead ends are not created by the opposition; they are created either by other characters or by general circumstances. For example, your lead must find some money he has buried in order to clear his name. When he arrives at the place where he buried the money, he finds a newly built housing development. Course of action blocked; tension increased.

Get Rid of Some Characters

Just as you can eliminate courses of action for your lead, you can also eliminate people who might help your lead. These people can even be viewpoint characters.

Focus on One Road

As people and courses of action that could help your lead achieve the story goal vanish, have your lead come to realize that success lies down one road and one road alone. This technique increases your reader's worry even further: If the lead can't succeed this way, she's lost!

• Tie up loose ends, unresolved questions, in the end segment of your novel. Loose ends are not story lines; they are simply matters that have been left up in the air and should be answered now so your readers aren't left hanging on any issues.

• The end of your novel is where you resolve all of your viewpoint characters' story lines, from the lead's main story line and subplot down to the least important viewpoint character's story line. The Blueprint takes care of this for you, but still it's helpful to know that the least important story lines are always resolved first, starting with the lowest "other character" and working up to the highest "other character." Then come the lead's subplot, the lead's main story line (which also resolves the opposition's story line and the confidant's story line) and, last of all, the romantic involvement's story line. The romantic thread—the coming together of lead and romantic involvement—always wraps up the book.

Here are some tips for resolving your story's various story lines:

Other Characters' Story Lines: Whether your other viewpoint characters achieve their story goals is completely up to you. Go with your writer's instincts. What feels right for your story? What would be most dramatic? The most moving? Would any of these characters achieving their story goals affect the lead in his quest? You can even kill off a viewpoint character if that feels right. The death of a viewpoint character can be the closing of one of the lead's doors to success—a limiting of options.

Lead's Subplot: If your novel contains a romantic involvement, then this romantic thread was your lead's subplot. And since the lead and the romantic involvement always end the story together, the romantic involvement wins, which means that in this respect the lead loses. But it's a happy loss, because by the end of the novel, the lead will have come to see that he loves the romantic involvement after all and wants to make that commitment.

If your novel does not contain a romantic involvement, you can resolve this story line in whatever feels right to you. The lead may either achieve this goal or not. Having the lead *not* achieve the subplot goal can add poignancy and realism to a story. In this case, if you wish, the novel may reflect life: You win some, you lose some.

Lead's Main Story Line: In popular commercial fiction, the lead nearly always achieves the story goal. In the Marshall Plan, he *always* does. A happy ending is a must. Readers must be able to see the lead they've been caring and worrying about and cheering for win. This is their payoff for hanging in there with your book.

Opposition and Confidant's Story Lines: When your lead wins, your opposition, who has consistently opposed your lead, of course loses. On the other hand, the confidant, who has consistently supported the lead, wins along with her.

Romantic Involvement's Story Line: The romantic involvement always ends up with the lead, which means the romantic involvement always ends up achieving his story goal.

Though the Blueprint takes care of these points for you, you should still be aware that at the novel's climax, the lead will move through four key plot points as he confronts the opposition for a final showdown:

1. The Worst Failure, the failure phase of an action section, in which the most devastating failure of the entire book is perpetrated by the opposition.

2. The Point of Hopelessness, a reaction section in response to the Worst Failure, in which it appears that all is lost and that there is no possible way the lead can achieve the story goal. This point in the story is often called the dark or black moment.

3. The Saving Act, the action the lead takes as a result of the analysis she did in the Point of Hopelessness—an action that miraculously reverses the entire course of the story, putting the lead suddenly in a position to vanquish the opposition and achieve the story goal. This action section is the only one in the novel in which the opposition *fails*.

4. The Wrap-Up, in which the lead first says and does what would be natural for him to say or do after finally achieving the story goal and setting life back on a normal happy course, and then, if your novel contains a romantic involvement, gets the gal or guy. (Here's where they walk hand in hand into the sunset.)

Story Surprises

Readers love to be kept in a perpetual state of worry as they read a novel. That's what suspense is all about. Another important element readers value in a story is surprise—the event or revelation they didn't see coming.

Why Are Surprises So Appealing?

Surprises please readers for a number of reasons.

• Surprises tell the reader that, thanks to an especially accomplished author, these special features are added into the story for extra entertainment value. Surprises are fun!

• Surprises remind the reader that there may be other information that hasn't yet been revealed and that the reader had better stay on her figurative toes.

• Surprises give a novel a lifelike complexity. A surprise that consists of a shocking development demonstrates that the novel, like life, probably won't go the way the reader expects.

• A surprise that consists of the revelation of shocking or unexpected information demonstrates that the novel, like life, is not a simple, one-layered recounting of events, but a complex, multilayered "world" in which there's more to what's going on than meets the eye . . . in which not all information is allowed to bubble to the surface at the same time.

• Surprises, unsurprisingly, prevent a story from dragging or becoming boring, a novel's cardinal sin.

The Best Surprises Are Planned

There's no limit to the number of surprises you can build into your novel. But every novel should incorporate at least three: surprises #1, #2 and #3. The Marshall Plan allows for easier insertion of surprises because it helps the writer completely plot the novel before writing it. The writer can see the "big picture" easily and can view the novel as an entire organism and decide what kinds of surprises will be most effective. It's far easier to build surprises into a novel before it's written than to suddenly dream one up as you're writing, then have to go back and plant any information or clues that will make this surprise possible.

What's a Surprise?

A surprise is an important, shocking story development that puts a whole new spin on your lead's pursuit of the story goal *and* makes the lead's chances of achieving the story goal appear slimmer.

A surprise occurs as the failure component of an action section. Surprises #1, #2 and #3, to be precise, occur in the action sections at the end of your novel's beginning, at the midpoint of your novel and at the end of your novel's middle, respectively.

A surprise must:

• Raise the stakes for your lead.

• Always be about your lead's main story line—her pursuit of the story goal.

- Be believable in light of what has occurred to your lead in the novel thus far.
- Must be worse than all preceding surprises.

As you work your way through the Blueprint and come to the three surprise points, use the Surprise Worksheets on pages 147–152 to conceive and weigh various possibilities to decide on the most effective surprises possible.

Surprise Worksheet—Surprise #1

To recap: At this point in my story, my lead's situation with respect to achieving the story goal is

_____

_____

_____

_____

_____

_____

_____

In this action section, my lead's short-term goal is to _____

_____

_____

_____

_____

_____

The following are possible, believable failures that might occur at the end of this action section:

Failure . . .	The effect of this failure on my lead's pursuit of the story goal would be . . .
• **A horrible or shocking discovery my lead makes?** • **Revelation of new information that is dire news for my lead in terms of achieving the story goal?** • **An action by the section's opposing character that negatively affects my lead?** • **Information that means my lead's efforts and beliefs about how best to achieve the story goal have been all wrong?**	
Example: Charles reveals that Walter didn't really die of a heart attack; he was poisoned.	Tina realizes the information he's after is far more important than she thought.

(Continued on next page.)

1. _____

2. _____

3. _____

4. _____

5. _____

6. _____

7. _____

8. _____

9. _____

10. _____

Of all the above failure possibilities, the one I find most interesting, that takes my story in a direction I would like it to go, is #_____.

Surprise Worksheet—Surprise #2

To recap: At this point in my story, my lead's situation with respect to achieving the story goal is

_____

_____

_____

_____

_____

_____

_____

In this action section, my lead's short-term goal is to _____

_____

_____

_____

_____

_____

The following are possible, believable failures that might occur at the end of this action section:

Failure . . .	The effect of this failure on my lead's pursuit of the story goal would be . . .
• **A horrible or shocking discovery my lead makes?** • **Revelation of new information that is dire news for my lead in terms of achieving the story goal?** • **An action by the section's opposing character that negatively affects my lead?** • **Information that means my lead's efforts and beliefs about how best to achieve the story goal have been all wrong?**	
Example: Charles reveals that Walter didn't really die of a heart attack; he was poisoned.	Tina realizes the information he's after is far more important than she thought.

(Continued on next page.)

1.

_____

2.

_____

3.

_____

4.

_____

5.

_____

6.

_____

7.

_____

8.

_____

9.

_____

10.

Of all the above failure possibilities, the one I find most interesting, that takes my story in a direction I would like it to go, is #_____.

Surprise Worksheet—Surprise #3

To recap: At this point in my story, my lead's situation with respect to achieving the story goal is

_____

_____

_____

_____

_____

_____

_____

In this action section, my lead's short-term goal is to _____

_____

_____

_____

_____

_____

The following are possible, believable failures that might occur at the end of this action section:

Failure . . .	The effect of this failure on my lead's pursuit of the story goal would be . . .
• **A horrible or shocking discovery my lead makes?** • **Revelation of new information that is dire news for my lead in terms of achieving the story goal?** • **An action by the section's opposing character that negatively affects my lead?** • **Information that means my lead's efforts and beliefs about how best to achieve the story goal have been all wrong?**	
Example: Charles reveals that Walter didn't really die of a heart attack; he was poisoned.	Tina realizes the information he's after is far more important than she thought.

(Continued on next page.)

1. _____

   _____

2. _____

   _____

3. _____

   _____

4. _____

   _____

5. _____

   _____

6. _____

   _____

7. _____

   _____

8. _____

   _____

9. _____

   _____

10. _____

    _____

Of all the above failure possibilities, the one I find most interesting, that takes my story in a direction I would like it to go, is #_____.

CHAPTER 17

How to Use the Marshall Plan Blueprint

H ere, at last, we get to the Marshall Plan Blueprint itself, a unique tool for plotting your novel.

How to Use the Marshall Plan Blueprint

For the most part, the Blueprint is self-explanatory, guiding you step-by-step through the plotting process. Before you begin, however, read the ten guidelines that follow for important additional information.

1. The Blueprint requires that you know the target word length for your novel, and (related to this) how many viewpoint characters your novel will have. Refer to pages 25 and 112 for this information. For your convenience, transfer it to the lines below.

The target word length for my novel is _____ words.
My novel will contain _____ viewpoint characters.

2. You may write directly in the workbook (a pencil—with a good eraser—is highly recommended!). When the Blueprint instructs you to insert additional section sheets, photocopy either the blank action section sheet on page 156 or the blank reaction section sheet on page 157, according to what you need. I would advise you to make multiple copies of each blank sheet ahead of time, so that as you're plotting you can readily take what you need from this supply, without having to interrupt the creative flow.

Simply insert the blank sheets into the Blueprint after the numbering charts. To keep things clear, you may want to draw a line through the charts once you've used them. You may also want to draw lines through section sheets in the Blueprint that you won't be needing.

3. In the Blueprint, the beginning, middle and end segments are numbered separately. The number charts tell you how to number the blank sheets you insert.

4. Carefully follow the "Go to" instructions at the bottom of the section sheets. Doing so is vital to your success with the Blueprint.

5. When you add blank sheets, the decision as to whether to use action section sheets or reaction section sheets is up to you, based on how your story is evolving.

6. If necessary, review chapter fifteen to remind yourself how the section sheets work.

7. If necessary, review chapter fourteen to remind yourself how to interweave your viewpoint characters' story lines. Unless the Blueprint explicitly tells you which viewpoint character to make the subject of a section, this decision is also up to you.

8. Pay careful attention to the Writing Coach column included on each of the Blueprint's section sheets. This special feature provides you with important instructions on how to complete the section sheets, as well as other tips and reminders.

9. For the sake of clarity, the pages of the Blueprint are designated with the letter B (for Blueprint) and a number. Use these numbers to move easily from page to page.

10. It's highly unlikely that you'll complete the whole process of plotting with the Blueprint in one session; in fact, I would urge you to take your time so you do your best, most careful work. When you end a session, mark your place with a bookmark so that you'll know exactly where you were when you begin work again.

Now turn to page 158, B1, the first page of the Blueprint. Good luck!

PART V

The Blueprint

Action

Section Character:

Where:

When:

Goal from
Character's
Last Section

Against

Conflict

Failure (Unless
Opposition)

New Goal
(OR Go to a
Reaction
Section)

	Reaction
Section Character:	
Where:	
When:	
	Failure from Character's Last Action Section
	With
	Emotional
	Rational
	New Goal

Action	[BEGINNING] #1	Writing Coach
	SECTION CHARACTER:	◄ Lead.
	Where:	Normal, day-to-day setting.
	When:	
		◄ What lead is doing just before the crisis hits.
Against		◄ The person or circumstance that brings about the crisis.
Conflict		◄ The occurrence of the crisis itself.
Failure		◄ Lead's inability to undo or deny the crisis.
	Go to B2.	

B2

Writing Coach	[BEGINNING] #2	Reaction
Lead. ▶	SECTION CHARACTER:	
	Where:	
Right after ▶ section #1	When:	
Briefly restate ▶ exactly what terrible thing has just happened to lead and what it means to her/him.		Failure from Character's Last Action Section
		With
Describe lead's ▶ emotional response to the crisis.		Emotional
Describe lead's ▶ analyzing and option-weighing process.		Rational
Lead's story goal. ▶		Story Goal
Lead's section goal ▶ that begins the pursuit of the story goal.		Section Goal
	Go to B3.	

Action	[BEGINNING] #3	Writing Coach
	SECTION CHARACTER:	◄ Lead.
	Where:	
	When:	
Goal from Character's Last Section		◄ Carry over lead's section goal from B2.
Against		◄ The character lead will confront in trying to achieve the section goal.
Conflict		◄ Outline the main points of the struggle between the two characters.
Failure		◄ Show lead failing to achieve the section goal.
New Goal		◄ Lead's new section goal as a result of the failure.
	Go to B4.	

B4

Action	[BEGINNING] #4	Writing Coach
	SECTION CHARACTER:	◄ Lead.
	Where:	
	When:	
Goal from Character's Last Section		◄ None, because this section starts lead's subplot.
Against		◄ Romantic involvement if you have one; another character if you don't.
Conflict		◄ Outline the main points of the struggle between the two characters.
Failure		◄ Show lead failing to achieve the section goal.
New Goal		◄ Lead's new section goal as a result of the failure.
	Go to B5.	

Action	**[BEGINNING] #5**	**Writing Coach**
	SECTION CHARACTER:	◄ Lead.
	Where:	
	When:	
Goal from Character's Last Section		◄ Carry over lead's section goal from B3.
Against		◄ The character lead will confront in trying to achieve the section goal.
Conflict		◄ Outline the main points of the struggle between the two characters.
Failure		◄ Show lead failing to achieve the section goal.
New Goal		◄ Lead's new section goal as a result of the failure.
	Go to B6.	

B6

Action	[BEGINNING] #6	Writing Coach
	SECTION CHARACTER:	◄ Viewpoint character #2.
	Where:	
	When:	
Goal from Character's Last Section		◄ None, because this starts VP character #2's story line.
Against		◄ The character VP character #2 will confront in trying to achieve the section goal.
Conflict		◄ Outline the main points of the struggle between the two characters.
Failure (Unless Opposition)		◄ If VP character #2 is opposition, show this character achieving the section goal; otherwise, show the character failing to achieve the section goal.
New Goal		◄ VP chracter #2's new section goal.
	Go to B7.	

Action	[BEGINNING] #7	Writing Coach
	SECTION CHARACTER:	◀ Lead.
	Where:	
	When:	
Goal from Character's Last Section		◀ Carry over the new goal from B4.
Against		◀ The character lead will confront in trying to achieve the section goal.
Conflict		◀ Outline the main points of the struggle between the two characters.
Failure		◀ Show lead failing to achieve the section goal.
New Goal		◀ Lead's new section goal as a result of the failure.

If your novel will have two viewpoint characters, go to B16.
Otherwise, go to B8.

B8

Action	[BEGINNING] #8	Writing Coach
	SECTION CHARACTER:	◄ Viewpoint character #3.
	Where:	
	When:	
Goal from Character's Last Section		◄ None, because this starts VP character #3's story line.
Against		◄ The character VP character #3 will confront in trying to achieve the section goal.
Conflict		◄ Outline the main points of the struggle between the two characters.
Failure		◄ Show VP character #3 failing to achieve the section goal.
New Goal		◄ VP character #3's new section goal as a result of the failure.

Go to B9.

Action	[BEGINNING] #9	**Writing Coach**
	SECTION CHARACTER:	◀ Lead.
	Where:	
	When:	
Goal from Character's Last Section		◀ Carry over new goal from B5.
Against		◀ The character lead will confront in trying to achieve the section goal.
Conflict		◀ Outline the main points of the struggle between the two characters.
Failure		◀ Show lead failing to achieve the section goal.
New Goal		◀ Lead's new section goal as a result of the failure.

If your novel will have three viewpoint characters, go to B16.
Otherwise, go to B10.

B10

Action	[BEGINNING] #10	Writing Coach
	SECTION CHARACTER:	◀ Viewpoint character #4.
	Where:	
	When:	
Goal from Character's Last Section		◀ None, because this starts VP character #4's story line.
Against		◀ The character VP character #4 will confront in trying to achieve the section goal.
Conflict		◀ Outline the main points of the struggle between the two characters.
Failure		◀ Show VP character #4 failing to achieve the section goal.
New Goal		◀ VP character #4's new section goal as a result of the failure.
	Go to B11.	

Action	[BEGINNING] #11	Writing Coach
	SECTION CHARACTER:	◀ Lead.
	Where:	
	When:	
Goal from Character's Last Section		◀ Carry over new goal from B7.
Against		◀ The character lead will confront in trying to achieve the section goal.
Conflict		◀ Outline the main points of the struggle between the two characters.
Failure		◀ Show lead failing to achieve the section goal.
New Goal		◀ Lead's new section goal as a result of the failure.

If your novel will have four viewpoint characters, go to B16.
Otherwise, go to B12.

B12

Action	[BEGINNING] #12	Writing Coach
	SECTION CHARACTER:	◀ Viewpoint character #5
	Where:	
	When:	
Goal from Character's Last Section		◀ None, because this starts VP character #5's story line.
Against		◀ The character VP character #5 will confront in trying to achieve the section goal.
Conflict		◀ Outline the main points of the struggle between the two characters.
Failure		◀ Show VP character #5 failing to achieve the section goal.
New Goal		◀ VP character #5's new section goal as a result of the failure.
	Go to B13.	

Action	[BEGINNING] #13	Writing Coach
	SECTION CHARACTER:	◄ Lead.
	Where:	
	When:	
Goal from Character's Last Section		◄ Carry over the new goal from B9.
Against		◄ The character lead will confront in trying to achieve the section goal.
Conflict		◄ Outline the main points of the struggle between the two characters.
Failure		◄ Show lead failing to achieve the section goal.
New Goal		◄ Lead's new section goal as a result of the failure.

If your novel will have five viewpoint characters, go to B16.
Otherwise, go to B14.

B14

Action	[BEGINNING] #14	Writing Coach
	SECTION CHARACTER:	◄ Viewpoint character #6.
	Where:	
	When:	
Goal from Character's Last Section		◄ None, because this starts VP character #6's story line.
Against		◄ The character VP character #6 will confront in trying to achieve the section goal.
Conflict		◄ Outline the main points of the struggle between the two characters.
Failure		◄ Show VP character #6 failing to achieve the section goal.
New Goal		◄ VP character #6's new section goal as a result of the failure.
	Go to B15.	

Action	**[BEGINNING] #15**	**Writing Coach**
	SECTION CHARACTER:	◄ Lead.
	Where:	
	When:	
Goal from Character's Last Section		◄ Carry over new goal from B11.
Against		◄ The character lead will confront in trying to achieve the section goal.
Conflict		◄ Outline the main points of the struggle between the two characters.
Failure		◄ Show lead failing to achieve the section goal.
New Goal		◄ Lead's new section goal as a result of the failure.
	Go to B16.	

B16

If your novel's word length will be . . .	Add . . .	And number them . . .
50,000–54,000 words	2 section sheets	[BEGINNING] #8 and #9
55,000–59,000 words	3 section sheets	[BEGINNING] #8 through #10
60,000–64,000 words	4 section sheets	[BEGINNING] #8 through #11
65,000–69,000 words	3 section sheets	[BEGINNING] #10 through #12
70,000–74,000 words	4 section sheets	[BEGINNING] #10 through #13
75,000–79,000 words	5 section sheets	[BEGINNING] #10 through #14
80,000–84,000 words	6 section sheets	[BEGINNING] #10 through #15
85,000–89,000 words	7 section sheets	[BEGINNING] #10 through #16
90,000–94,000 words	6 section sheets	[BEGINNING] #12 through #17
95,000–99,000 words	7 section sheets	[BEGINNING] #12 through #18
100,000–104,000 words	8 section sheets	[BEGINNING] #12 through #19
105,000–109,000 words	9 section sheets	[BEGINNING] #12 through #20
110,000–114,000 words	10 section sheets	[BEGINNING] #12 through #21
115,000–119,000 words	9 section sheets	[BEGINNING] #14 through #22
120,000–124,000 words	10 section sheets	[BEGINNING] #14 through #23
125,000–129,000 words	11 section sheets	[BEGINNING] #14 through #24
130,000–134,000 words	12 section sheets	[BEGINNING] #14 through #25
135,000–139,000 words	13 section sheets	[BEGINNING] #14 through #26
140,000–144,000 words	12 section sheets	[BEGINNING] #16 through #27
145,000–149,000 words	13 section sheets	[BEGINNING] #16 through #28
150,000–154,000 words	14 section sheets	[BEGINNING] #16 through #29

Go to B18

How to Number Surprise #1

If your novel's word length will be . . .	Number Surprise #1 . . .
50,000–54,000 words	[BEGINNING] Section Sheet #10
55,000–59,000 words	[BEGINNING] Section Sheet #11
60,000–64,000 words	[BEGINNING] Section Sheet #12
65,000–69,000 words	[BEGINNING] Section Sheet #13
70,000–74,000 words	[BEGINNING] Section Sheet #14
75,000–79,000 words	[BEGINNING] Section Sheet #15
80,000–84,000 words	[BEGINNING] Section Sheet #16
85,000–89,000 words	[BEGINNING] Section Sheet #17
90,000–94,000 words	[BEGINNING] Section Sheet #18
95,000–99,000 words	[BEGINNING] Section Sheet #19
100,000–104,000 words	[BEGINNING] Section Sheet #20
105,000–109,000 words	[BEGINNING] Section Sheet #21
110,000–114,000 words	[BEGINNING] Section Sheet #22
115,000–119,000 words	[BEGINNING] Section Sheet #23
120,000–124,000 words	[BEGINNING] Section Sheet #24
125,000–129,000 words	[BEGINNING] Section Sheet #25
130,000–134,000 words	[BEGINNING] Section Sheet #26
135,000–139,000 words	[BEGINNING] Section Sheet #27
140,000–144,000 words	[BEGINNING] Section Sheet #28
145,000–149,000 words	[BEGINNING] Section Sheet #29
150,000–154,000 words	[BEGINNING] Section Sheet #30

B18

Action	[BEGINNING] #___ (Surprise #1)	**Writing Coach** See B17 for numbering instructions
	SECTION CHARACTER:	◄ Lead.
	Where:	
	When:	
Goal from Character's Last Section		◄ Carry over the new goal from B13.
Against		◄ The character lead will confront in trying to achieve the section goal.
Conflict		◄ Outline the main points of the struggle between the two characters.
Failure— Surprise #1		◄ Show lead failing devastatingly to achieve the section goal. Worst failure yet: raises stakes; sheds new light on story goal; spins story in a new direction. For surprise ideas, use Surprise Worksheet— Surprise #1 (page 147).
	Go to B19.	

B19

Writing Coach	[MIDDLE] #1	*Reaction*
Lead. ▶	SECTION CHARACTER:	
	Where:	
Right after ▶ surprise #1.	When:	
Briefly restate ▶ exactly what terrible thing has just happened to lead and what it means to her/him.		Failure from Character's Last Action Section
		With
Describe lead's ▶ emotional response to the surprise #1.		Emotional
Describe lead's ▶ analyzing and option-weighing process.		Rational
Lead's new section ▶ goal as a result of the analysis.		New Goal
	Go to B20.	

B20

If your novel's word length will be . . .	Add . . .	And number them . . .
50,000–54,000 words	8 section sheets	[MIDDLE] #2 through #9
55,000–59,000 words	9 section sheets	[MIDDLE] #2 through #10
60,000–64,000 words	10 section sheets	[MIDDLE] #2 through #11
65,000–69,000 words	11 section sheets	[MIDDLE] #2 through #12
70,000–74,000 words	12 section sheets	[MIDDLE] #2 through #13
75,000–79,000 words	13 section sheets	[MIDDLE] #2 through #14
80,000–84,000 words	14 section sheets	[MIDDLE] #2 through #15
85,000–89,000 words	15 section sheets	[MIDDLE] #2 through #16
90,000–94,000 words	16 section sheets	[MIDDLE] #2 through #17
95,000–99,000 words	17 section sheets	[MIDDLE] #2 through #18
100,000–104,000 words	18 section sheets	[MIDDLE] #2 through #19
105,000–109,000 words	19 section sheets	[MIDDLE] #2 through #20
110,000–114,000 words	20 section sheets	[MIDDLE] #2 through #21
115,000–119,000 words	21 section sheets	[MIDDLE] #2 through #22
120,000–124,000 words	22 section sheets	[MIDDLE] #2 through #23
125,000–129,000 words	23 section sheets	[MIDDLE] #2 through #24
130,000–134,000 words	24 section sheets	[MIDDLE] #2 through #25
135,000–139,000 words	25 section sheets	[MIDDLE] #2 through #26
140,000–144,000 words	26 section sheets	[MIDDLE] #2 through #27
145,000–149,000 words	27 section sheets	[MIDDLE] #2 through #28
150,000–154,000 words	28 section sheets	[MIDDLE] #2 through #29

Go to B22

How to Number Surprise #2

If your novel's word length will be . . .	Number Surprise #2 . . .
50,000–54,000 words	[MIDDLE] Section Sheet #10
55,000–59,000 words	[MIDDLE] Section Sheet #11
60,000–64,000 words	[MIDDLE] Section Sheet #12
65,000–69,000 words	[MIDDLE] Section Sheet #13
70,000–74,000 words	[MIDDLE] Section Sheet #14
75,000–79,000 words	[MIDDLE] Section Sheet #15
80,000–84,000 words	[MIDDLE] Section Sheet #16
85,000–89,000 words	[MIDDLE] Section Sheet #17
90,000–94,000 words	[MIDDLE] Section Sheet #18
95,000–99,000 words	[MIDDLE] Section Sheet #19
100,000–104,000 words	[MIDDLE] Section Sheet #20
105,000–109,000 words	[MIDDLE] Section Sheet #21
110,000–114,000 words	[MIDDLE] Section Sheet #22
115,000–119,000 words	[MIDDLE] Section Sheet #23
120,000–124,000 words	[MIDDLE] Section Sheet #24
125,000–129,000 words	[MIDDLE] Section Sheet #25
130,000–134,000 words	[MIDDLE] Section Sheet #26
135,000–139,000 words	[MIDDLE] Section Sheet #27
140,000–144,000 words	[MIDDLE] Section Sheet #28
145,000–149,000 words	[MIDDLE] Section Sheet #29
150,000–154,000 words	[MIDDLE] Section Sheet #30

B22

Action	[MIDDLE] #___ (Surprise #2)	Writing Coach See B21 for numbering instructions
	SECTION CHARACTER:	◀ Lead.
	Where:	
	When:	
Goal from Character's Last Section		◀ Carry over the new goal from last section about lead's main story line.
Against		◀ The character lead will confront in trying to achieve the section goal.
Conflict		◀ Outline the main points of the struggle between the two characters.
Failure—Surprise #2		◀ Show lead failing devastatingly to achieve the section goal. Worst failure yet: raises takes; sheds new light on story goal; spins story in a new direction. For surprise ideas, use Surprise Worksheet—Suprise #2 (page 149)
	Go to B23.	

If your novel's word length will be . . .	Add . . .	And number them . . .
50,000–54,000 words	9 section sheets	[MIDDLE] #11* through #19
55,000–59,000 words	10 section sheets	[MIDDLE] #12* through #21
60,000–64,000 words	11 section sheets	[MIDDLE] #13* through #23
65,000–69,000 words	12 section sheets	[MIDDLE] #14* through #25
70,000–74,000 words	13 section sheets	[MIDDLE] #15* through #27
75,000–79,000 words	14 section sheets	[MIDDLE] #16* through #29
80,000–84,000 words	15 section sheets	[MIDDLE] #17* through #31
85,000–89,000 words	16 section sheets	[MIDDLE] #18* through #33
90,000–94,000 words	17 section sheets	[MIDDLE] #19* through #35
95,000–99,000 words	18 section sheets	[MIDDLE] #20* through #37
100,000–104,000 words	19 section sheets	[MIDDLE] #21* through #39
105,000–109,000 words	20 section sheets	[MIDDLE] #22* through #41
110,000–114,000 words	21 section sheets	[MIDDLE] #23* through #43
115,000–119,000 words	22 section sheets	[MIDDLE] #24* through #45
120,000–124,000 words	23 section sheets	[MIDDLE] #25* through #47
125,000–129,000 words	24 section sheets	[MIDDLE] #26* through #49
130,000–134,000 words	25 section sheets	[MIDDLE] #27* through #51
135,000–139,000 words	26 section sheets	[MIDDLE] #28* through #53
140,000–144,000 words	27 section sheets	[MIDDLE] #29* through #55
145,000–149,000 words	28 section sheets	[MIDDLE] #30* through #57
150,000–154,000 words	29 section sheets	[MIDDLE] #31* through #59

*A reaction section: lead's response to surprise #2.

Go to B25.

How to Number Surprise #3

If your novel's word length will be . . .	Number Surprise #3 . . .
50,000–54,000 words	[MIDDLE] Section Sheet #20
55,000–59,000 words	[MIDDLE] Section Sheet #22
60,000–64,000 words	[MIDDLE] Section Sheet #24
65,000–69,000 words	[MIDDLE] Section Sheet #26
70,000–74,000 words	[MIDDLE] Section Sheet #28
75,000–79,000 words	[MIDDLE] Section Sheet #30
80,000–84,000 words	[MIDDLE] Section Sheet #32
85,000–89,000 words	[MIDDLE] Section Sheet #34
90,000–94,000 words	[MIDDLE] Section Sheet #36
95,000–99,000 words	[MIDDLE] Section Sheet #38
100,000–104,000 words	[MIDDLE] Section Sheet #40
105,000–109,000 words	[MIDDLE] Section Sheet #42
110,000–114,000 words	[MIDDLE] Section Sheet #44
115,000–119,000 words	[MIDDLE] Section Sheet #46
120,000–124,000 words	[MIDDLE] Section Sheet #48
125,000–129,000 words	[MIDDLE] Section Sheet #50
130,000–134,000 words	[MIDDLE] Section Sheet #52
135,000–139,000 words	[MIDDLE] Section Sheet #54
140,000–144,000 words	[MIDDLE] Section Sheet #56
145,000–149,000 words	[MIDDLE] Section Sheet #58
150,000–154,000 words	[MIDDLE] Section Sheet #60

B25

Action	[MIDDLE] #___ (Surprise #3)	Writing Coach See B24 for numbering instructions
	SECTION CHARACTER:	◄ Lead.
	Where:	
	When:	
Goal from Character's Last Section		◄ Carry over the new goal from last section about lead's main story line.
Against		◄ The character lead will confront in trying to achieve the section goal.
Conflict		◄ Outline the main points of the struggle between the two characters.
Failure— Surprise #3		◄ Show lead failing devastatingly to achieve the section goal. Worst failure yet: raises stakes; sheds new light on story goal; spins story in a new direction. For surprise ideas, use Surprise Worksheet— Suprise #3 (page 151)
	Go to B26.	

B26

Writing Coach	[END] #1	Reaction
Lead. ▶	SECTION CHARACTER:	
	Where:	
Right after ▶ surprise #3.	When:	
Briefly restate ▶ exactly what terrible thing has just happened to lead and what it means to her/him.		Failure from Character's Last Action Section
		With
Describe lead's ▶ emotional response to suprise #3.		Emotional
Describe lead's ▶ analyzing and option-weighing process.		Rational
Lead's new section ▶ goal as a result of the analysis.		New Goal
	Go to B27.	

If your novel's word length will be . . .	Add . . .	Then go to . . .
50,000–54,000 words	2 section sheets	B36 if you have *no* romantic involvement. B51 if you have a romantic involvement.
55,000–59,000 words	3 section sheets	
60,000—64,000 words	4 section sheets	
65,000–69,000 words	5 section sheets	B34 if you have *no* romantic involvement. B49 if you have a romantic involvement.
70,000–74,000 words	6 section sheets	
75,000–79,000 words	7 section sheets	
80,000–84,000 words	8 section sheets	
85,000–89,000 words	9 section sheets	
90,000–94,000 words	10 section sheets	B32 if you have *no* romantic involvement. B47 if you have a romantic involvement.
95,000–99,000 words	11 section sheets	
100,000–104,000 words	12 section sheets	
105,000–109,000 words	13 section sheets	
110,000–114,000 words	14 section sheets	
115,000–119,000 words	15 section sheets	B30 if you have *no* romantic involvement. B45 if you have a romantic involvement.
120,000–124,000 words	16 section sheets	
125,000–129,000 words	17 section sheets	
130,000–134,000 words	18 section sheets	
135,000–139,000 words	19 section sheets	
140,000–144,000 words	20 section sheets	B28 if you have *no* romantic involvement. B43 if you have a romantic involvement.
145,000–149,000 words	21 section sheets	
150,000–154,000 words	22 section sheets	

B28

Action	[END] Ending Sequence Countdown—15th from the End	Writing Coach
	SECTION CHARACTER:	◀ Lead.
	Where:	
	When:	
Goal from Character's Last Section		◀ Carry over the new goal from last section about lead's subplot.
Against		◀ The character lead will confront in trying to achieve the section goal.
Conflict		◀ Outline the main points of the struggle between the two characters.
Failure		◀ Show lead failing to achieve the section goal.
New Goal		◀ Lead's new section goal as a result of the failure.
	Go to B29.	

Action	[END] Ending Sequence Countdown—14th from the End	Writing Coach
	SECTION CHARACTER:	◀ Viewpoint character #6.
	Where:	
	When:	
Goal from Character's Last Section		◀ Carry over the new goal from last section about VP character #6's story line.
Against		◀ The character VP character #6 will confront in trying to achieve the section goal.
Conflict		◀ Outline the main points of the struggle between the two characters.
Final Failure or Success		◀ Resolve VP character #6's story line—fails or succeeds in achieving story goal.

Go to B30.

B30

Action	[END] Ending Sequence Countdown—13th from the End	Writing Coach
	SECTION CHARACTER:	◄ Lead.
	Where:	
	When:	
Goal from Character's Last Section		◄ Carry over the new goal from last section about lead's main story line.
Against		◄ The character lead will confront in trying to achieve the section goal.
Conflict		◄ Outline the main points of the struggle between the two characters.
Failure		◄ Show lead failing to achieve the section goal.
New Goal		◄ Lead's new section goal as a result of the failure.
	Go to B31.	

Action	[END] Ending Sequence Countdown—12th from the End	Writing Coach
	SECTION CHARACTER:	◄ Viewpoint character #5.
	Where:	
	When:	
Goal from Character's Last Section		◄ Carry over the new goal from last section about VP character #5's story line.
Against		◄ The character VP character #5 will confront in trying to achieve the section goal.
Conflict		◄ Outline the main points of the struggle between the two characters.
Final Failure or Success		◄ Resolve VP character #5's story line—fails or succeeds in achieving story goal.
	Go to B32.	

B32

Action	[END] Ending Sequence Countdown—11th from the End	Writing Coach
	SECTION CHARACTER:	◄ Lead.
	Where:	
	When:	
Goal from Character's Last Section		◄ Carry over the new goal from last section about lead's subplot.
Against		◄ The character lead will confront in trying to achieve the section goal.
Conflict		◄ Outline the main points of the struggle between the two characters.
Failure		◄ Show lead failing to achieve the section goal.
New Goal		◄ Lead's new section goal as a result of the failure.
	Go to B33.	

Action	[END] Ending Sequence Countdown—10th from the End	Writing Coach
	SECTION CHARACTER:	◄ Viewpoint character #4.
	Where:	
	When:	
Goal from Character's Last Section		◄ Carry over the new goal from last section about VP character #4's story line.
Against		◄ The character VP character #4 will confront in trying to achieve the section goal.
Conflict		◄ Outline the main points of the struggle between the two characters.
Final Failure or Success		◄ Resolve VP character #4's story line— fails or succeeds in achieving story goal.
	Go to B34.	

B34

Action	[END] Ending Sequence Countdown—9th from the End	Writing Coach
	SECTION CHARACTER:	◄ Lead.
	Where:	
	When:	
Goal from Character's Last Section		◄ Carry over the new goal from last section about lead's main story line.
Against		◄ The character lead will confront in trying to achieve the section goal.
Conflict		◄ Outline the main points of the struggle between the two characters.
Failure		◄ Show lead failing to achieve the section goal.
New Goal		◄ Lead's new section goal as a result of the failure.
	Go to B35.	

Action	[END] Ending Sequence Countdown—8th from the End	Writing Coach
	SECTION CHARACTER:	◄ Confidant.
	Where:	
	When:	
Goal from Character's Last Section		◄ Carry over the new goal from last section about confidant's story line.
Against		◄ The character confidant will confront in trying to achieve the section goal.
Conflict		◄ Outline the main points of the struggle between the two characters.
Failure		◄ Show confidant failing to achieve the section goal.
New Goal		◄ Confidant's new section goal as a result of the failure.
	Go to B36.	

B36

Action	[END] Ending Sequence Countdown—7th from the End	Writing Coach
	SECTION CHARACTER:	◄ Lead.
	Where:	
	When:	
Goal from Character's Last Section		◄ Carry over the new goal from last section about lead's subplot.
Against		◄ The character lead will confront in trying to achieve the section goal.
Conflict		◄ Outline the main points of the struggle between the two characters.
Final Failure or Success		◄ Resolve lead's sub-plot—fails or succeeds in achieving subplot goal.
	Go to B37.	

Action	[END] Ending Sequence Countdown—6th from the End	Writing Coach
	SECTION CHARACTER:	◀ Opposition.
	Where:	
	When:	
Goal from Character's Last Section		◀ Carry over the new goal from last section about opposition's story line.
Against		◀ The character opposition will confront in trying to achieve the section goal.
Conflict		◀ Outline the main points of the struggle between the two characters.
Success		◀ Show opposition succeeding in achieving the section goal.
New Goal		◀ Opposition's new section goal.
	Go to B38.	

B38

Action	[END] Ending Sequence Countdown—5th from the End	Writing Coach
	SECTION CHARACTER:	◄ Lead.
	Where:	
	When:	
Goal from Character's Last Section		◄ Carry over the new goal from last section about lead's main story line.
Against		◄ The character lead will confront in trying to achieve the section goal.
Conflict		◄ Outline the main points of the struggle between the two characters.
Failure		◄ Show lead failing to achieve the section goal.
New Goal		◄ Lead's new section goal as a result of the failure.
	Go to B39.	

Action	[END] Ending Sequence Countdown—4th from the End	Writing Coach
	SECTION CHARACTER:	◄ Lead.
	Where:	
	When:	
Goal from Character's Last Section		◄ Carry over the new goal from B38.
Against		◄ Opposition.
Conflict		◄ Outline the main points of the struggle between lead and opposition. The most serious confrontation between them yet— the final showdown.
Worst Failure		◄ Show lead failing to achieve the section goal—a terrible defeat.
	Go to B40.	

B40

Writing Coach	[END] Ending Sequence Countdown—3rd from the End	*Reaction*
Lead. ▶	SECTION CHARACTER:	
	Where:	
Right after B39. ▶	When:	
Briefly restate ▶ exactly what terrible thing has just happened to lead and what it means to her/him.		Failure from Character's Last Action Section
		With
Describe lead's ▶ emotional response to the Worst Failure. All appears lost: Point of Hopelessness.		Emotional
Describe lead's ▶ analyzing and option-weighing process.		Rational
Lead's section goal ▶ as a result of the analysis. A sudden, brilliant new idea!	Go to B41.	New Goal

Action	[END] Ending Sequence Countdown—2nd from the End	Writing Coach
	SECTION CHARACTER:	◄ Lead.
	Where:	
	When:	
Goal from Character's Last Section		◄ Carry over the new goal from B40.
Against		◄ Opposition.
Conflict		◄ Outline the main points of the struggle between lead and opposition. At the end, lead executes idea from B40—Saving Act.
Success		◄ Resolve lead's main story line— succeeds in achieving story goal!
	Go to B42.	

B42

Writing Coach	[END] Ending Sequence Countdown—The End	Reaction
Lead. ▶	SECTION CHARACTER:	
	Where:	
	When:	
Briefly restate ▶ exactly what wonderful thing has just happened to lead and what it means to her/him.		Success from Character's Last Action Section With
Describe lead's ▶ emotional response to the success. Briefly show lead ▶ living life restored to normal. Stop.		Emotional

Action	[END] Ending Sequence Countdown—15th from the End	Writing Coach
	SECTION CHARACTER:	◀ Lead.
	Where:	
	When:	
Goal from Character's Last Section		◀ Carry over the new goal from last section about lead's subplot.
Against		◀ Romantic involvement.
Conflict		◀ Outline the main points of the struggle between lead and romantic involvement.
Failure		◀ Show lead failing to achieve the section goal.
New Goal		◀ Lead's new section goal as a result of the failure.
	Go to B44.	

B44

Action	[END] Ending Sequence Countdown—14th from the End	Writing Coach
	SECTION CHARACTER:	◄ Viewpoint character #6.
	Where:	
	When:	
Goal from Character's Last Section		◄ Carry over the new goal from last section about VP character #6's story line.
Against		◄ The character VP character #6 will confront in trying to achieve the section goal.
Conflict		◄ Outline the main points of the struggle between the two characters.
Final Failure or Success		◄ Resolve VP character #6's story line—fails or succeeds in achieving story goal.
	Go to B45.	

Action	[END] Ending Sequence Countdown—13th from the End	Writing Coach
	SECTION CHARACTER:	◀ Lead.
	Where:	
	When:	
Goal from Character's Last Section		◀ Carry over the new goal from last section about lead's main story line.
Against		◀ The character lead will confront in trying to achieve the section goal.
Conflict		◀ Outline the main points of the struggle between the two characters.
Failure		◀ Show lead failing to achieve the section goal.
New Goal		◀ Lead's new section goal as a result of the failure.
	Go to B46.	

B46

Action	[END] Ending Sequence Countdown—12th from the End	Writing Coach
	SECTION CHARACTER:	◄ Viewpoint character #5.
	Where:	
	When:	
Goal from Character's Last Section		◄ Carry over the new goal from last section about VP character #5's story line.
Against		◄ The character VP character #5 will confront in trying to achieve the section goal.
Conflict		◄ Outline the main points of the struggle between the two characters.
Final Failure or Success		◄ Resolve VP character #5's story line—fails or succeeds in achieving story goal.
	Go to B47.	

Action	[END] Ending Sequence Countdown—11th from the End	Writing Coach
	SECTION CHARACTER:	◀ Lead.
	Where:	
	When:	
Goal from Character's Last Section		◀ Carry over the new goal from last section about lead's subplot.
Against		◀ Romantic involvement.
Conflict		◀ Outline the main points of the struggle between lead and romantic involvement.
Failure		◀ Show lead failing to achieve the section goal.
New Goal		◀ Lead's new section goal as a result of the failure.
	Go to B48.	

B48

Action	[END] Ending Sequence Countdown—10th from the End	Writing Coach
	SECTION CHARACTER:	◀ Confidant.
	Where:	
	When:	
Goal from Character's Last Section		◀ Carry over the new goal from last section about confidant's story line.
Against		◀ The character confidant will confront in trying to achieve the section goal.
Conflict		◀ Outline the main points of the struggle between the two characters.
Failure		◀ Show confidant failing to achieve the section goal.
New Goal		◀ Confidant's new section goal as a result of the failure.
	Go to B49.	

Action	[END] Ending Sequence Countdown—9th from the End	Writing Coach
	SECTION CHARACTER:	◄ Lead.
	Where:	
	When:	
Goal from Character's Last Section		◄ Carry over the new goal from last section about lead's main story line.
Against		◄ The character lead will confront in trying to achieve the section goal.
Conflict		◄ Outline the main points of the struggle between the two characters.
Failure		◄ Show lead failing to achieve the section goal.
New Goal		◄ Lead's new section goal as a result of the failure.
	Go to B50.	

B50

Action	[END] Ending Sequence Countdown—8th from the End	Writing Coach
	SECTION CHARACTER:	◄ Opposition.
	Where:	
	When:	
Goal from Character's Last Section		◄ Carry over the new goal from last section about opposition's story line.
Against		◄ The character opposition will confront in trying to achieve the section goal.
Conflict		◄ Outline the main points of the struggle between the two characters.
Success		◄ Show opposition succeeding in achieving the section goal.
New Goal		◄ Opposition's new section goal.
	Go to B51.	

Action	[END] Ending Sequence Countdown—7th from the End	Writing Coach
	SECTION CHARACTER:	◄ Lead.
	Where:	
	When:	
Goal from Character's Last Section		◄ Carry over the new goal from last section about lead's subplot.
Against		◄ Romantic involvement.
Conflict		◄ Outline the main points of the struggle between lead and romantic involvement.
Failure		◄ Show lead failing to achieve the section goal.
New Goal		◄ Lead's new section goal as a result of the failure.

Go to B52.

B52

Action	[END] Ending Sequence Countdown—6th from the End	Writing Coach
	SECTION CHARACTER:	◀ Romantic involvement.
	Where:	
	When:	
Goal from Character's Last Section		◀ Carry over the new goal from last section about romantic involvement's story line.
Against		◀ The character romantic involvement will confront in trying to achieve the section goal.
Conflict		◀ Outline the main points of the struggle between the two characters.
Failure		◀ Show romantic involvement failing to achieve the section goal.
New Goal		◀ Romantic involvement's new section goal as a result of the failure.

Go to B53.

Action	[END] Ending Sequence Countdown—5th from the End	Writing Coach
	SECTION CHARACTER:	◄ Lead.
	Where:	
	When:	
Goal from Character's Last Section		◄ Carry over the new goal from last section about lead's main story line.
Against		◄ The character lead will confront in trying to achieve the section goal.
Conflict		◄ Outline the main points of the struggle between the two characters.
Failure		◄ Show lead failing to achieve the section goal.
New Goal		◄ Lead's new section goal as a result of the failure.
	Go to B54.	

B54

Action	[END] Ending Sequence Countdown—4th from the End	Writing Coach
	SECTION CHARACTER:	◀ Lead.
	Where:	
	When:	
Goal from Character's Last Section		◀ Carry over the new goal from B53.
Against		◀ Opposition.
Conflict		◀ Outline the main points of the struggle between lead and opposition. The most serious confrontation yet—the final showdown.
Worst Failure		◀ Show lead failing to achieve the section goal—a terrible defeat.
	Go to B55.	

Writing Coach	[END] Ending Sequence Countdown—3rd from the End	*Reaction*
Lead ▶	SECTION CHARACTER:	
	Where:	
	When:	
Briefly restate ▶ exactly what wonderful thing has just happened to lead and what it means to her/him.		Success from Character's Last Action Section
		With
Describe lead's ▶ emotional response to the Worst Failure. All appears lost: Point of Hopelessness.		Emotional
Describe lead's ▶ analyzing and option-weighing process.		Rational
Lead's new section ▶ goal as a result of the analysis. A sudden, brilliant new idea!		New Goal
	Go to B56.	

B56

Action	[END] Ending Sequence Countdown—2nd from the End	Writing Coach
	SECTION CHARACTER:	◄ Lead.
	Where:	
	When:	
Goal from Character's Last Section		◄ Carry over the new goal from B55.
Against		◄ Opposition.
Conflict		◄ Outline the main points of the struggle between lead and opposition. At the end, lead executes idea from B55—Saving Act.
Success		◄ Resolve lead's main story line— succeeds in achieving story goal!
	Go to B57.	

Writing Coach	[END] Ending Sequence Countdown—The End	*Reaction*
Lead. ▶	SECTION CHARACTER:	
	Where:	
	When:	
Briefly restate ▶ exactly what wonderful thing has just happened to lead and what it means to her/him.		Success from Character's Last Action Section
		With
Describe lead's ▶ emotional response to the success. Briefly show lead ▶ living life restored to normal.		Emotional
RESOLVE ▶ romantic thread— lead and romantic involvement commit to each other.		
	Stop.	

PART VI

Writing From the Blueprint

CHAPTER 18

The Five Fiction Modes

How do you actually *write* good fiction? You've got a strong story, well plotted from start to finish. Now it's time to translate your Blueprint story into an actual manuscript.

When writers I work with or teach ask me how to write effective fiction prose, I recommend that they become familiar with five modes of fiction writing as I have defined them: action, summary, dialogue, feelings/thoughts and background. I advise you to do the same. Once you've mastered each mode and know how to write well in it, all you have to do is make sure you're always in one specific mode as you're writing. Doing this ensures that at all times you know what you're doing and why. The mosaic created by piecing together these passages written in various modes is a tight, well-written novel.

First let's take a look at each mode; then we'll discuss how to put them together.

Action Mode

Action is the mode in which you'll write most of your novel. It's the mode used to present real-time action in a story. Events are presented in strict chronological order as they happen. Every action is presented.

Keep a few points in mind as you write in action mode.

Present Events One at a Time, in True Chronological Order

Though in life events often occur simultaneously, you must accept the fact that in fiction, which is after all a linear art form—a line of words—all of life's actions are broken down far enough until they can be presented one at a time.

For this reason, in action mode you would never write:

He ducked as the saber whipped toward him.

Instead you'd write:

The saber whipped toward him. He ducked.

He would have had no reason to duck if the saber hadn't whipped toward him. Clearly, the whipping of the saber precedes the ducking.

Because presenting events one at a time is so important in fiction writing, you should, in almost all cases, eschew *as* and *while*. Only if two events are truly happening simultaneously should you write them that way:

Chomping on her gum, Alexandra got up and left the room.

"I'd love a doughnut," Patty said, taking one.

The one-at-a-time, chronological concept is easy to implement once you get the hang of it. Mastering this mode alone will do wonders for the quality of your writing. Beginners unfamiliar with this concept perpetrate such atrocities as:

Running to the window, Justin saw Mrs. Jones stomping up
the front walk.

Elliott let out a shriek as the bullet pierced his chest.

Rose petted the lazy cat, smiling as it purred.

A writer familiar with correct action-mode writing would have written:

Justin ran to the window and saw Mrs. Jones stomping up
the front walk.

The bullet pierced Elliott's chest. He let out a shriek.

Rose petted the lazy cat. It purred. She smiled.

Some writers, when I tell them about action-mode writing, protest that sometimes events, though they indeed happen one at a time, happen so close together that to present them one at a time instead of simultaneously strikes them as strange—as if presenting them one at a time puts too much time between the events. The previous sentence about poor Elliott is an example.

Don't worry about that. Closely spaced events presented one at a time don't strike readers that way. One thing at a time. Trust me.

Employ Action/Result Writing

Related to the previous concept is action/result writing, another important component of correct action-mode writing. Very often an event (an action) causes another event (the result). These, too, must be presented chronologically.

Justin wouldn't have seen Mrs. Jones (result) if he hadn't run to the window (action). Elliott wouldn't have shrieked (result) if the bullet hadn't pierced his chest (action). Rose wouldn't have smiled (result) if the cat hadn't purred (action). The cat wouldn't have purred (result) if Rose hadn't petted it (action).

When you combine the concept of one-at-a-time/chronological with action/result, it's hard to make a mistake in action mode.

Don't Summarize

Do not summarize any events when you're writing in action mode. When you summarize events, you're in summary mode, and you should be aware that you have switched modes. Here's an example of writing that's in action mode but slides into summary mode without the author even being aware of it:

Cara typed the letter for Mr. Loehman and placed it in the folder. She went to the kitchen, poured herself some coffee and returned to her desk. Ricki had left her some bills of lading to file. Cara filed them in the cabinet behind her chair. Then she finished her work.

ACTION MODE

INADVERTENT SUMMARY

Summary Mode

There are places when you should use summary mode, but you should be aware that you are switching into it and you should know the reason why. Summary mode should be used sparingly because it distances the reader. You're not showing us what characters are doing, you're telling us in a removed way that may make readers feel uninvolved—not an effect to strive for.

When you're in summary mode, you report events in a condensed, synoptic, narrative form. Following are the legitimate uses of summary mode.

To Report **Some** *Story Events*

Some story events don't require detailed description, such as routine activities we're all familiar with. Some might argue that all the details of Cara's desk work could just as well have been delivered in summary mode. If the actual details of her desk work don't matter, summary mode is fine. The point is whether the details matter to the story you're telling. Out of context, we can't answer this question about Cara's work.

However, there are some activities that few would argue must be related in detail: cleaning the refrigerator, going to the bathroom (usually not even mentioned at all—one of those fiction conventions we've grown used to), washing your hands, getting dressed.

If the details matter to the telling of your story, by all means report them. In the end, it's up to you, as is the level of detail you get down to. In one novel, every single thing Cara does at her desk might be important. In another, it would be enough to go to the extreme other end of the detail spectrum and say, "Cara worked all afternoon." It all boils down to what's relevant to the story you're telling.

To Telescope Story Time

To make a passage of time in which nothing relevant to your story happens pass quickly, summary mode comes in extremely handy.

The last three weeks of school passed in a flurry of activity.

Summary is also useful to report events that happen regularly or over a long period of time.

Each morning for the next week she saw him behind the security desk in the lobby, and every time she passed him he nodded once and gave her a big, handsome smile.

To Emphasize Emotion Instead of Events

This technique applies to writing a reaction section. Sometimes a novelist wants to show a character's emotional state during a period of time, without relating the character's actions during that time. For example:

> During the month Kevin was in Cincinnati, Sherry wandered about the apartment, not doing much of anything except eating, sleeping and watching TV. She'd never been so lonely in her life.

Dialogue Mode

Many teachers of writing include dialogue in action writing, but I don't. Dialogue has so many rules of its own, and it plays such a vital role in the novel, that to me it is a mode of its own.

What are these rules?

Dialogue Must Advance Your Plot in Some Way

Though you needn't ignore the fact that people do digress and engage in small talk, for the most part your dialogue should pertain to the story at hand. For example, if you're writing an action section in which your viewpoint character and another character argue, the argument should be about the viewpoint character trying to achieve his short-term goal. The argument shouldn't move into any other unrelated areas, like old resentments about other matters.

In all cases, avoid needless chitchat or repetition, though both are common in real-life dialogue. Keep your dialogue tight and to the point. Use it mostly as a vehicle by which characters convey information.

Keep Dialogue Natural-Sounding

I say natural-sounding rather than natural, because dialogue in fiction usually bears little resemblance to the slack, undisciplined chatter of real life. What you're trying to do is create the *illusion* of natural. How?

• Don't let a character blather on for too long. People don't go around delivering monologues and soliloquies in real life, and these sound even stranger on the printed page. Some writers set a three-sentence limit. They don't let a character go on uninterrupted for longer than that. At the very least, after three sentences they introduce a gesture or "piece of business," simply to break things up. You needn't adhere rigidly to this rule, but you get the idea.

• Use contractions for characters who would realistically use them. Most people do. Dialogue without at least some contractions reads stiffly and artificially.

• One of the sections on your Character Fact Lists is Distinctive Speech Pattern. The whole point of defining this trait is to recognize that we all speak differently. Make an effort not only to incorporate a character's distinctive speech pattern often, but also work in general to keep characters sounding different, as people do in real life.

• Eliminate words when appropriate. ("Hear that?")

• Vary sentence length in your dialogue; this also adds realism.

There's one way in which some beginning writers carry authenticity too far, and that is in the use of dialect. Though dialect was once in fashion, it's not today. Often it's considered politically incorrect, and it runs the risk of offending some readers. If you have a character who speaks in a highly accented, idiosyncratic way, suggest it as best you can through your word choice, rather than going to great lengths to transcribe it exactly.

Today's readers would inevitably trip on the following line of dialogue, from *Toby Tyler* by James Otis (1939):

> "Yes, I s'pose so, myself; but, you see, I don't expect that's
> the name that belongs to me. But the fellers call me so, an'
> so does Uncle Dan'l."

A novelist today would probably leave "fellers," since "fellows" would be too stilted, and write out the rest:

> "Yes, I suppose so myself, but you see, I don't expect that's
> the name that belongs to me. But the fellers call me so, and
> so does Uncle Daniel."

The word choices alone convey the way Toby speaks.

Go Easy on the Dialogue Tags

Dialogue tags are speaker attributions: "he said," "she asked." Most writers use more of them than necessary. You need them mostly to help the reader keep straight who's speaking.

Moreover, the words *said, asked, answered* and the like are in almost all cases not only sufficient but preferable. They have become transparent to readers. Don't resort to imaginative replacements for these words (*hissed, rasped, husked* and other words of this type that once gave romance writers a bad name). Use other words only when you must to convey how something is said.

> "Quick!" she whispered. "Look over there."

A speaker's words themselves should in most cases convey how they're spoken. Sometimes they can't, and a *said* replacement is called for:

> "You're such a rat," she cooed.

Or

> "You're such a rat," she said with a loving smile.

Speaking of tags, the old-fashioned "said Marjorie" and "asked Bill" look strange to some readers today. Stick with "Marjorie said" and "Bill asked."

Sometimes you don't even need a tag. Just end a line of dialogue, and begin a sentence about the speaker.

> "How many times do I have to tell you?" Gladys grabbed the brooch out of Oliver's hand. "You are *not* to touch my things!"

Use Body Language Sparingly

New writers sprinkle their dialogue with a lot of gestures and mannerisms. Characters smile, grin, frown, shake their head, shrug their shoulders, raise their eyebrows, shake and sigh. They nod a lot.

These new writers believe that readers must know everything a character is doing and every expression that appears on his face as he is speaking. The truth is, most of the time readers don't really care, unless the gesture or mannerism is important for conveying meaning.

Keep body language to a minimum in your dialogue. They don't add to dialogue, and there's nothing intrinsically interesting about them. What's more, many aren't necessary because the words have already delivered the message. Consider:

> He nodded eagerly. "Oh, yes, Aunt Martha!"

> Colleen looked away uninterestedly. "I really couldn't care less."

Both examples are redundant. Each one delivers the same message twice. Always choose dialogue over a gesture, if you have a choice.

One instance in which a gesture can come in handy is when you need a small pause for dramatic effect within a character's dialogue.

> "I couldn't leave Belinda. Not after all she's done for me— medical school, raising our kids." **Frank looked down at his cigarette, studied it a moment, then gave Susan a frank look.** "I love you more than anyone in the world, but I can't marry you."

When Mixing Dialogue With a Character's Feelings/ Thoughts and Gestures, Use F-A-D Order

Sometimes as you're writing dialogue you'll find that a gesture or gestures can only go one place. In Frank's dialogue above, for example, the sentence containing his body language must go there for dramatic impact.

Other times when a writer may not be so certain, the F-A-D rule comes in handy. F-A-D refers to the correct order in which to present the three elements of dialogue mode:

> **F** eeling/thought
>
> **A** ction
>
> **D** ialogue

This is the logical order for these three elements. A feeling or thought does come first, and we nearly always make some sort of gesture before we then speak.

Feeling	Action	Dialogue
A violent chill passed through him.	His hand shook.	"But Margo died a year ago."

You don't always need all three components. Sometimes one isn't necessary; for example, a character's feelings might be made perfectly clear by his action. At other times there *is* no action to show.

Whatever the reason, if you leave out a component, present the remaining components in the correct order:

Action	Dialogue
His hand shook.	"But Margo died a year ago."

Feeling	Dialogue
A violent chill passed through him.	"But Margo died a year ago."

Keep Dialogue Exchanges Separate

Have your characters ask each other questions and reply to them one at a time.

Not:

"Did you get any sleep last night?" Rachel asked. "Are you having trouble getting to school so early?"

"Yeah, I went to bed around eleven. No, I don't think starting school at seven is so bad."

But:

"Did you get any sleep last night?" Rachel asked.

"Yeah, I went to bed around eleven."

"Are you having trouble getting to school so early?"

"No, I don't think starting school at seven is so bad."

The first version reads awkwardly because too many questions have been posed at once, and then they're both answered at the same time. In the second version, a question is posed, it's answered, another question is posed, *it's* answered. Action-reaction-action-reaction. One thing at a time.

Start a New Paragraph Each Time You Switch Characters

Every time you begin a line about a different character, press "enter." Readers have been trained to recognize that a new paragraph means a new person is talking (if a conversation has no dialogue tags, the paragraphing is the reader's only means of keeping the participants straight). But it's a good habit to start a fresh paragraph for anything you write about a new character.

The following passage does not convey the meaning the author intended:

"Did you see how fast Gregory went down that slide?" Gloria laughed. "He's a daredevil!"

This is what the author actually meant (the passage describes two people):

"Did you see how fast Gregory went down that slide?"
Gloria laughed.
"He's a daredevil!"

The reader knows that line one is about character one, line two is about Gloria, and line three is about character one again.

Use Adverbs Judiciously

Don't kill every adverb in your dialogue, but use them sparingly. Often they're unnecessary ("she whispered softly" or "he yelled loudly").

Whenever possible, let your words convey how they're spoken. If the words as you've written them don't perform this function, can you rewrite them so that they do?

"Poor little thing," Angelo said sadly.

Could become

"Poor little thing. My heart breaks for him."

In some cases an adverb is necessary to convey to the reader that words are not being spoken as the reader would expect.

"You hate your mother!" she said teasingly.

Likewise, it's necessary to use an adverb when you want to convey that a character's words are not being spoken in the way the reader would expect:

"I'm going to kill myself," she said flatly.

Summarize When Appropriate

Within dialogue mode it is sometimes appropriate and desirable to summarize. New writers often summarize dialogue for no reason. Dialogue that's summarized when it shouldn't be yanks the reader a level away from your story. You're telling the reader what your people are saying, not letting the reader hear for himself. Below you'll find the correct reasons to summarize dialogue.

When the Reader Really Doesn't Need the Exact Words

Once in a while a character explains something to another character, but the reader needn't hear the exact explanation either because it doesn't really matter or because the reader already knows.

SUMMARIZED
DIALOGUE

"This will be your desk. Now come in here, please." Nancy led the way into a small mail room. "Over here's the Xerox machine and right here's the postal meter." She demonstrated how they worked.

When Dialogue Is Routine or Mundane

Some exchanges of dialogue are so familiar to us that to include them in your novel word for word is unnecessary. The classic example is one or more characters ordering in a restaurant.

> "Don't you just love this place?" Laura gazed around her at the hanging plants and warm red brick.
>
> "I can't help associating it with Rick," Jordan said. "This was our place."
>
> A waiter appeared, and they ordered salads.   ⟵ SUMMARIZED DIALOGUE
>
> Laura placed her hand over Jordan's and pressed it. "I know it hurts, babe."

Another example is telephone *hellos* and *good-byes*. These are so routine and dull that you needn't include them at all:

> On an impulse she dialed Hank.
>
> "Why are you calling me?" He sounded irritated, as if he was in the middle of something important.
>
> "I . . . just wanted to tell you Taylor's recital is on Saturday morning. Eight o'clock at the academy."
>
> "All right," he said, his voice kinder now. "Thanks."
>
> Putting down the phone, Rita began to cry.

When the Dialogue Is Relating Something the Reader Already Knows

Once in a while a character will tell another character something the reader has already seen or heard about. In these cases it's appropriate—and desirable, to avoid boring repetition—to summarize dialogue.

> Harrigan threw himself into his chair with a great sigh. He turned to Kartsev. "You went to see the old lady?"
>
> Kartsev nodded.
>
> "OK, what'd you get?"
>
> Kartsev told him what Mrs. Zimmermann had said about the man in the alley last night.   ⟵ SUMMARIZED DIALOGUE
>
> Harrigan jotted a few notes on his pad.

Feelings/Thoughts Mode

There are two ways to convey your characters' feelings and thoughts. The way favored by most editors and readers is to state the thought or feeling, using "she thought," "he wondered" or the like only when absolutely necessary for clarity.

> Brian looked at the trolley piled high with dirty dishes. It would take him all night to wash them all. He'd never make it to Alexa's party.

If you're conveying a character's actual thought, simply write it, without italics unless they're necessary for clarity.

> Daniel stepped to the edge of the cliff and gazed down upon the plantation, with its gleaming white house and lush old trees. I love this place more than I can say. I'll do anything to stay alive and come back to it.
>
> He turned, got back on his horse and headed for the railroad station.

If a character is remembering dialogue, put it in italics:

> Thalia glanced in each direction to make sure Mr. Kaspar wasn't around. Then she took the key to the jewelry case from the pocket of her skirt and, as quietly as she could, unlocked its sliding glass door. What was it Mr. Kaspar had said? *This necklace, the one with the sapphires in the center, is the most valuable piece I've ever had in the store.* Slowly Thalia reached for it.

Background Mode

Beginners have the most trouble with this mode.

Every novel must convey background information to the reader so the present story will make sense. Yet it must be used sparingly and in small pieces, because although it's important, it's also inherently dull. It stops the movement of the story, which readers hate.

The trick is to supply background information to your readers in such a way that they're barely aware they're getting it. How?

Reduce It

Writers nearly always find they need to convey less background information than they at first thought. You'll never convey every piece of information on a Character Fact List. Don't even try. Instead, take the opposite approach: How *little* background information can you get away with telling the reader and still have your story make sense?

Ideally, background information should be supplied when it's relevant, at the time that it's needed to explain something that's happening in your story. Ask yourself, Would my reader understand this passage without background information? If the answer is "no," provide what's necessary, but no more.

> Adrian walked slowly down the corridor, looking at the children's artwork taped to the walls. One group consisted of drawings of a small pink pig having various adventures. Adrian smiled. Mrs. Columbo had said she was going to show the children *Babe* and then have them draw pictures about it.

Don't Repeat It

Explain something to your reader only once. If you're afraid he or she will miss it, the way to prevent this isn't to repeat it; instead, make more of it when you present it. For example, bring it out in a conversation and have a character react with surprise. Even if your reader does miss an explanation, chances are he or she will realize this and flip back in the book to look for it.

Keep Readers Unenlightened

Beginners often believe that if we don't know everything about a character, we won't care what happens to him or her. This is untrue. If you create a connection between a character and your reader by making the character sympathetic or interesting, the reader will come along, trusting that eventually all necessary explanation will be provided.

In fact, many of our most accomplished novelists intentionally withhold information, knowing that unanswered questions will make the reader turn pages. Haven't you read novels in which a viewpoint character's deep dark secret isn't revealed until well into the story?

Chop It Up

The worst sin a novelist can commit is to write page after page of background information about a character at the beginning of the novel. Some try to lessen the effects of this technique by starting with the novel's present story, then presenting pages of background. It doesn't help. Background should rarely be presented this way, at the beginning of the book or anywhere else. Readers hate it.

If you really must tell the reader a lot about a character's background, boil it down to its essentials (see Reduce It, page 229) and then spoon-feed it in small bites.

Convert It

This is by far the best method. Often you can present background information by transforming it into other modes.

Action

A character's actions in the present story can tell us a lot about her past. A young man who frowns darkly at the deep end of the pool at the YMCA, then refuses to get on the diving board, makes it pretty clear that at some point in his past he had an unpleasant diving experience and that he is afraid to try again. This may be all we need to know.

Dialogue

People explain things to each other all the time. Rather than simply tell us that Frances has had trouble in the romance department and has just broken up with her boyfriend, find a way to have her realistically tell all this to another character (the confidant?). Just be careful not to go overboard with this technique, creating the kind of artificial conversations that sound as if they belong on a stage. This kind of stagey dialogue signals to the reader that you are simply using the dialogue as a vehicle to convey information, which is as bad as just giving us the information straight out.

If Absolutely Necessary, Create a Flashback

Flashbacks have been the subject of much controversy. Some editors dislike them so much that they forbid their authors to employ them. Why? A flashback is background information told as an actual section that took place before the present story. Many readers dislike them because they bring the present story to a prolonged halt.

A flashback is only necessary when, for some reason, it's important to show the reader exactly how something before the story happened—who did what, who said what, what was thought and felt. If you create one, structure it as an action section with all of an action section's components.

To give the flashback more immediacy, use the past perfect tense (those *had*s you've heard are anathema to fiction) a couple of times to slide the reader into the flashback, and a couple more to slide the reader out. In the flashback itself, use the simple past tense.

Get It Over With

Get all of your background information out of the way by the end of your novel's beginning. Background is part of your story's setup. Once the reader has entered your novel's middle, the core of the story, he or she won't gladly put up with any story stoppers.

Creating the Mosaic

Now that you know the five fiction writing modes, be "mode aware" as you're writing. If you're cognizant of what mode you're in, you won't accidentally do something that's wrong for that mode. Always have a reason to switch modes; in fact, you should have a reason for everything you do in your novel.

At first, if it's helpful, you might want to color-code your writing by modes, using different colored highlighters. If you don't want to color in entire passages, outline them. The objective is to make yourself aware of the various modes and how you're combining them to form fiction prose.

Starting on page 232 you'll find a portion of a mode-marked page from a novel manuscript. We're in an action section, and the story goal of the viewpoint character, a young woman named Julia, is to find her missing brother Dave. In this section her goal is to catch up with Professor Kuroff, the last person known to have seen Dave.

Since this book isn't in color, brackets have been used instead.

Julia ran up to the store window. It was a jewelry store. She peered inside. Professor Kuroff stood at the counter, speaking to a young man about a watch lying between them. She hurried into the store and approached the professor.

ACTION

"Excuse me, Professor Kuroff—"

He spun around, his face darkly furious. "I am busy, young woman, can't you see that?" He spoke with a thick Eastern European accent. He turned back to the clerk.

DIALOGUE

"Professor, I just need to ask you a question. It's my brother, Dave. Dave Anderson. He's missing and you were the last person to see him."

Professor Kuroff's shoulders in his heavy wool coat hunched up, and he turned with a great exasperated groan and stomped out, pushing past Julia.

ACTION

"He left his watch!" the young man said.

"I'll give it to him."

DIALOGUE

Julia grabbed the watch and ran outside. She looked to her right, then to her left, and saw the professor starting down the stairs to the subway. She ran after him. He threw a hunted look over his shoulder and ran faster down the stairs.

ACTION

Julia followed, descending to the subway.

SUMMARY

How long had it been since she'd taken the subway? She'd promised herself never again, but now she had no choice.

FEELINGS/ THOUGHTS

She bought a token and hurried through the turnstile to the platform. A train stood at the edge, its doors open. She ran toward it and spotted Professor Kuroff sitting against the wall opposite, to the right of the door. He saw her and his eyes widened in horror.

She held up his watch.

At first he looked confused; then he glanced at his wrist and his mouth opened in further outrage, but at that moment the subway doors began to slide shut.

ACTION

Julia made it to the doors just before they met and reached out to put her arm through the space.

Instantly, as if from nowhere, a police officer appeared and grabbed her arm, pulling it back. The doors met and the train began to slide down the track.

"You don't understand," Julia said. "My brother is missing and that man on the train was the last person to see him. Also"—she held the watch in front of the officer's face—"he left this in the jewelry store."

DIALOGUE

The officer stared at her as if she were crazy, then shook his head and walked away. "Go home, miss."

DIALOGUE

Julia hurried to edge of the platform, just in time to see the end of the train disappearing into the dark tunnel. She stomped her foot. She held the photo out in front of her, and pocketed the watch.

ACTION

Without meaning to, she gazed down onto the littered track. Suddenly she could feel a strong arm pushing at her back, could feel herself falling, flying out into nothingness, could see the trash rushing up to meet her, feel the stark coldness of the metal against her face.

BACKGROUND

Everything around her back to spin. She felt hot all of a sudden; weird black shapes swam before her eyes. Then everything went black.

ACTION

CHAPTER 19

Sections

You now have at your disposal all the tools you need to write professional-quality fiction. However, as you convert your section sheets into actual written sections, there are some points to keep in mind.

Tips for Writing the Action Section

Writers often ask me how long an action section should be when it's written out. There's no hard and fast rule. An action section containing a prolonged and intricate conflict could run fifteen pages. An action section that is one of a string of fast-moving action sections in which a character is in a high-pressure distress situation could run half a page.

A section is not a scene! The Marshall Plan does not use the scene concept. A section is a unit of story action in which a viewpoint character pursues *one* short-term goal. A character who has fallen through the ice into a freezing-cold lake and can't find the hole to crawl out again would most likely have as her short-term goal, find that hole. This action section, then, when written out, might be only a paragraph long—a taut, suspenseful paragraph, but a paragraph nonetheless.

All that said, because everyone likes a rule of thumb, I do answer the question by saying that the average section, written out, runs five to six typed, double-spaced pages.

How to Start

Write just enough to set up the section. Immediately make it clear who your viewpoint character is. Nothing is more annoying than wading through several paragraphs before we know who a section is about. Then establish the section's time and place.

Time

Refer to "When" on your section sheet. Follow these guidelines:

1. If the section just before this one featured the same viewpoint

character, you might have to state the time relative to the time of that last section.

> At four o'clock that afternoon, she was on the West Side Highway . . .
>
> Twenty minutes later, Trevor knocked on Porcella's door . . .
>
> The following morning . . .

2. However, even if the section just before this one featured the same viewpoint character, you won't have to state the time at all if this new action follows immediately on the heels of the previous action.

Failure from Previous Section	Start of New Section
but couldn't see the hole he'd fallen through.	His lungs aching, he groped the underside of the ice until . . .

3. If the section just before this one did *not* feature this viewpoint character, you'll have to state the time of this new section.

> On Thursday, just before noon, Marguerite entered the shipyard by the north gate.

> Two weeks after her meeting with Jane, Michiko took the train from New Haven to New York.

> Friday morning dawned bright and clear, a perfect day for the picnic.

You don't have to get fancy when you state the time. It's an anchor the reader needs to orient himself in your story. Just state it right away, plainly and simply, so that your reader can get his bearings and move on to the important stuff.

Place

Refer to "Where" on the section sheet. The guidelines for stating the place, the setting of the section, are similar to those for stating the time.

1. Even if the section just before this one featured the same viewpoint character, if the character has moved, you must tell the reader this.

At Rosie's, he took a seat at the far end of the bar so he could watch the door.

Marsha's house was a real dump.

Driving ninety on Route 1, Justin flicked on the radio and turned it all the way up.

2. If the section just before this one featured the same viewpoint character, and this action is occurring in the same place, obviously you needn't restate the location.

3. If the section just before this one did *not* feature this viewpoint character, state where this new section is taking place.

Bring the Reader Up-to-Date

Once you've established the time and location of this section (if necessary), bring the reader up-to-date about anything that has happened to your viewpoint character since his last section that will in any way affect him in this section. Life goes on in the intervals between a character's sections, and in nearly all cases this time must be accounted for. Ideally, anything that's happened during this time wasn't about the character seeking her story goal. However, the reader may still need to know about it.

> At ten-thirty that night, almost immediately after the show, Graham pushed his way out into the alley and was immediately blinded by flashbulbs. *Damn.* **He and Ericson had had a heated argument about this. Graham had told him to make sure security kept this alley clear.** Now he'd be on the front page of every tabloid in the supermarket.

Usually you'll present this updating information in background mode, as in the previous example.

Updating is also handy when you want to begin a section at the verge of the conflict, but things have happened right up to this moment that the reader should know about.

> An hour later Alicia sat in Beverly Stewart's vast office. The door opened and Alicia looked up. Beverly walked into the

room in her confident gait. She wore a deep mauve pant suit of brushed silk. She saw Alicia and stopped, her eyes growing wide with surprise.

"How the hell did you get in here?"

"It was easy." **Actually, Alicia had had to slip the custodian a twenty before he'd let her up the back staircase. Then she'd simply marched past Mrs. Stewart's bulldog of a secretary, saying Mrs. Stewart was expecting her.**

If Necessary, Restate the Section Goal

Consider whether the reader already knows your viewpoint character's section goal. This is important. The reader must have a clear grasp of what your character is after.

If this character's last section was a reaction section, the goal of this section would have been stated there. If many sections featuring other characters followed, the reader may have forgotten what this character decided. Remind the reader.

Obviously, you don't keep directly stating section goals. "She had to get Monty to agree to the divorce." "He must find that money before Vinnie got here." You state the goal through the character's actions or dialogue.

"How the hell did you get in here?"

"It was easy." Actually, Alicia had had to slip the custodian a twenty before he'd let her up the back staircase. Then she'd simply marched past Mrs. Stewart's bulldog of a secretary, saying Mrs. Stewart was expecting her.

"What do you want?" Mrs. Stewart sat down at her desk.

Alicia leveled her a threatening glare. **"I want you to stop seeing my husband."**

Feelings/thoughts mode is also used frequently to convey the viewpoint character's section goal.

Randy ran out of the woods and down the slope. The plant was surrounded by a chain-link fence at least twelve feet high. **How would he ever get in?**

Give Us a Good Fight

Now dive into the conflict phase, the heart of the section. When you plotted the conflict, you made sure to get the most out of the situation you'd set up. Now, as you *write* this conflict, make sure your writing does the conflict justice. Don't rush. If on your section sheet you wrote, "Evelyn begs Irv to turn down the job in Dallas for Kimberly's sake," don't throw it away now with a couple of lines. Think hard about how you can write this as dramatically as possible.

Bring the Failure Down Hard

When you wrote your section sheet you dropped the failure like an anvil on your character's head. Be sure to write it that way now. No weak resistance on the opposing character's part; no slow dawning of failure in the viewpoint character's chase or escape. Whatever the failure is, write it so it has the strongest, most devastating impact on your viewpoint character possible. Whenever possible, have your characters chew up the scenery—stopping just short of melodrama.

On your section sheet you wrote: "Candace laughs, makes it clear she'd never go out with the likes of him."

In your actual section you write:

> Candace threw back her head and laughed heartily. Then she gave him a pitying look. "You're the sorriest excuse for a man I've ever seen. Look at you. Fat, bald, homely. I don't even let men who look like you clean my pool!" She leaned forward, her gaze menacing now. "Get out of here before I call an exterminator."

Tips for Writing the Reaction Section

How long should a written reaction section be? There's no one right length, but generally speaking, the average reaction section is a bit shorter than the average action section: four to five typed, double-spaced manuscript pages.

As in the action section, identify the viewpoint character, then anchor the reader in time and place if this is called for. If this reaction section is in response to the section just before it, the character hasn't changed locations and no time has passed, these anchors are of course unnecessary.

Be sure that in the writing of this section, as in the plotting of it, you make it clear what the failure the viewpoint character has just suffered means to him or her. You can achieve this in dialogue mode, for example, if another character is present (*With*), or in feelings/thoughts mode.

How to Convey Emotion

The emotional and rational phases of the reaction section are the most important; they are, after all, the whole point of having a reaction section in the first place. Many writers have difficulty conveying a character's strong emotions. They write, "Linda was outraged" or "Maxine was furious" or "June was despondent."

These fall flat because the writers are telling us about the characters' emotions, not showing us. We are expected to take their word for it that Linda is outraged, Maxine was furious or June was despondent. But we must see these emotions for ourselves. How can we "see" emotion? We see it through the actions the emotion induces. In fiction, emotion is—exclusively—as emotion does.

Simply have your character *physically* react, in a way that's realistic for him or her (refer to your Character Fact List, if necessary), to her feelings. Linda might scream and throw groceries at the wall. Maxine might quietly seethe while calling a friend to make deadly plans for revenge. June might crawl into bed, curl up and weep.

Make the emotion phase important in your reaction section. Don't throw it away. Emotion is one of the prime elements readers seek in a novel. It's what they'll remember most vividly after they finish reading yours.

The Analysis Phase

The length of the rational, or analysis, phase of the reaction section will depend on the nature of the failure the viewpoint character has just experienced. It will also depend on the number of options open to the character in terms of new action.

If you're writing a murder mystery or a suspense novel, for instance, and your lead is reacting to a failure having to do with an unidentified killer or stalker (the "invisible" opposition), your lead might discuss the events that have transpired thus far with the confidant, and this discussion might go on for some time. Do what's right for the story you're telling.

About Time

Beginning writers ask me a lot of questions relating to time in the reaction section.

At one extreme are questions relating to whether a reaction section can be brief. The answer is "yes." The only criterion for using a reaction section is that you want to show your reader the actual emotional and rational response to a failure. This response needn't be lengthy.

Let's say you're writing the end of your novel, the pace is relatively fast and your lead, who has been searching for his wife who disappeared (the crisis), discovers in a failure that his wife is being kept prisoner by a man he thought was his best friend. He's got a gun trained on the wife's head.

Though your lead must act quickly, he must first react emotionally and rationally to this devastating discovery. So here you would write a short but intense reaction section.

At the other extreme are questions as to whether a reaction section can cover *a lot* of time. The answer here is also "Yes." Time is flexible in the reaction section in a way that it's not in the action section. In the action section, summary is used very little because most of the events are presented in action and dialogue modes. In the reaction section, long periods of time may pass, as time often does when we're reacting to adverse circumstances.

You don't, however, want to *describe* all of this time. So you use summary mode to convey that time is passing, and focus on the character's emotional and rational responses as you do.

Joy cried a lot over the next few weeks, mostly whenever she looked at something that had belonged to Roger. Finally she pulled herself together and decided she had better get rid of his things. She packed them up, boxes and boxes, and called the Salvation Army to have them taken away. Once they were gone, she was able to think more clearly. | SUMMARY

What would she do with her life now that Roger was gone? What would she do with her *days*? When he was alive, she'd spent nearly all of her time helping him through his illness. Now no one needed her. She had no job, no family, no close friends. She realized that if she was to survive, she had better make some drastic changes in her life.

The first day of May, she made an appointment with a career counselor. | ACTION

The Joy of Viewpoint Writing

When you plotted your sections, you featured one viewpoint character in each, a person in pursuit of a short-term goal. The plotting centered on this quest. But how do you write a section so that it's clear to your readers who your viewpoint character is?

Filtered Prose

You use viewpoint writing. Viewpoint writing is writing through which everything is filtered through the senses and awareness of the viewpoint character. We see, hear, taste, smell, touch and know only what the viewpoint character does.

Viewpoint writing answers a lot of those questions that arise as you're writing. For instance: What should I describe? How much should I describe? How should I describe it? Viewpoint writing says that you describe what it would be natural for your viewpoint character to take note of; you go into as much detail as your viewpoint character would think about; and you describe everything through your viewpoint character's sensibilities.

If you're writing about a character going in to see her boss, you wouldn't write, "Lorraine knocked on the door of Miss Cicero, her boss," because obviously Lorraine knows who Miss Cicero is. You would write the sentence exactly as Lorraine would think it: "Lorraine knocked on Miss Cicero's door."

Whenever you're in doubt, submit your question to viewpoint writing. Your viewpoint character snoops in someone's medicine cabinet and finds rows of pill bottles. You give us the names of some of the medications. Do you tell us what they're for? Answer: If your viewpoint character knows what they're for, and it would be natural at this moment for him to think about that, yes. Otherwise, no.

The Voice of Viewpoint Writing

Using viewpoint writing means writing in the tone or "voice" of your viewpoint character. Two events through different viewpoint characters' sensibilities could read entirely differently.

> Lunch at The Four Seasons was exquisite, every bit as elegant as Greta had hoped it would be. Afterward, she took Cissy to see *The Lion King*, a darling musical version of the animated feature Greta loved to watch over and over back in Chicago.

They ate at some fancy overpriced place where the waiters never left you alone to eat in peace. When Cissy caught a glance at the bill she nearly pissed her pants right there at the table. Afterward, Greta took her to see a play about some stupid animal puppets dancing around on the stage.

Limited Awareness

In viewpoint writing, the author never "intrudes." This means you would never write, "She had no way of knowing that this would be the most important day of her life," or "Little did he know . . ." or " . . . because she was sound asleep and didn't hear Sonya pounding on the front door." If your viewpoint character doesn't know about it, we don't hear about it.

Another form of intrusion would be to write, "Amy got the fewest presents of all but played happily all Christmas day, for she was not a spoiled girl." Amy would not think about herself this way. This passage is in the voice of the author commenting on Amy's personality.

Living the Story

Viewpoint writing, when executed well, is what makes readers feel as if they are living a story right along with a viewpoint character. You have, in effect, placed your reader within the brain and body of your character.

Think about viewpoint writing as you read. You'll find novels in which the rules of this technique are broken, but you'll also find that these books don't involve you nearly so much as the books that follow these rules.

CHAPTER 20

Connectors

You now have your beads—your written sections—but you haven't strung them yet. Now it's time to do that, to join them so that they work together as effectively as possible. The way to do this is with connectors.

Connectors are devices for splicing sections together. There are three types of connectors.

The Space-Break Connector

When to use it:
1. When a section about one viewpoint character is followed by a section about *another* viewpoint character.
2. To signal the passage of time between two sections about the *same* viewpoint character.

How to do it:
At the end of the first section, press "enter" twice, leaving a space of one blank line. (If a space-break connector falls at the bottom or top of a manuscript page, indicate the space break with one centered asterisk.)

Examples:

1. Two different viewpoint characters

. . . Silently Brad turned the knob and pushed the door slowly open. A thick rotting smell assailed his nostrils and he drew back, grimacing. "Carrie?"

He moved into the room. Carrie lay on the bed, perfectly still. He approached her, his gaze fixed on her face.

It was clear she'd never answer his question, not today or ever.

{SPACE-BREAK CONNECTOR}

Penny hurried along the sidewalk, not even bothering to avoid the puddles. She checked her watch. It was nearly five-thirty. If she hurried she'd make it to the bank before Beatrice left for the day. . . .

2. Same viewpoint character

. . . Sarah picked up the flowers and buried her face in their sweetness. A card fell from them onto her desk. *Sarah—please don't give up on me now. I promise to try harder and make it work. I'll wait till six. If you don't come, I'll understand. Todd*

The clock on her desk said 5:20. She'd never make it home in time. But she wanted to. Yes, she wanted to very much. Frantically she dialed his number. That weird busy signal again. Damn it! Todd's phone was still out of order.

She yanked her sweater off the back of her chair and ran out of the office.

{SPACE-BREAK CONNECTOR}

The lights were on in Todd's apartment. Sarah ran past the doorman and jabbed at the elevator button. . . .

The Run-Together Connector

When to use it: When two sections (action-action, action-reaction, reaction-action) are about the same viewpoint character, and neither a dramatic break nor any connecting text is necessary.

How to do it: Simply run the text together, with no visible separation.

Example:

(Reaction-action)

. . . She no longer had any choice.

She had to confront Elgin Matthews. {RUN-TOGETHER CONNECTOR}

She slammed down her "Next Window, Please" sign on the counter in front of her and grabbed her coat from the hook. "Tell Jennifer I had to go," she said to Herman. "Family emergency."

The Summary Connector

When to use it: Between two sections about the same viewpoint character, where some bridging text would be helpful or natural.

How to do it: Create a passage—in summary mode, and no more than a few paragraphs—that takes the character from one section to the other.

Example:

". . . No, I won't tell you where I got it, and what's more, neither will Sean."

"We'll just see about that," Martha said, and walked out of the room.

She took Changebridge Road north and turned right onto 202. There was construction near the health club and she had to wait to get by. Finally she pulled into Sean's complex.

She used her key and walked in. Sean was on the phone, laughing. She grabbed the receiver from his hand and hung it up.

"Hey!"

You've Done It

Once you've completed all of our connectors, you have a complete novel that should, thanks to the Blueprint, come pretty close to your target word length. Only a few finishing touches are left to be done. You'll apply them in the next chapter.

CHAPTER 21

Final Touches

Your novel is almost ready to submit. Only a few finishing touches remain.

Chaptering

At this point your novel is more or less in the form of one long chapter. Chapters are arbitrary divisions, holdovers from the time when novels were run in installments in periodicals. But readers have come to expect them, and they do make a novel easier to put down and come back to. So chapter we will.

Where? The current fashion is to make chapters shorter than longer. Aim for an average of three sections per chapter, and let the following guidelines help you decide where to put the breaks. When you've made them all, start from the beginning and number your chapters.

Chaptering Guidelines
1. End chapter one at the end of section #1.
2. Insert a chapter break after the action sections containing surprise #1, surprise #2 and surprise #3.
3. Divide chapters at space-break connectors.
4. End chapters following action sections featuring your lead.

To make a break, simply insert your cursor at the spot in the text where one chapter will end and the next begin, and press "enter" until you're halfway down the following page. Center the chapter number two lines above the start of the text.

Length Adjustment

Having inserted your chapter breaks, you can now see how close your manuscript comes to your target word length. You recorded your target manuscript length on page 25. If the Blueprint did its job, you should be pretty near the mark. However, you no doubt run a bit over or under. Ideally, your manuscript should be within a range of ten pages above or below the prescribed number of manuscript pages.

Trim or add to bring your manuscript within this range. If your manuscript is too long, look for places to trim without losing any emotion or drama. For example, where you may have used a summary connector, you might substitute a space-break connector if doing so would not detract from your story. Conversely, if your manuscript is too short, see if there are places where you can lengthen the conflict phases of action sections or where you can play up the emotional phases in reaction sections.

Selecting a Title

Some writers can't work on a novel unless it has a title from the start. If you're one of these writers, ask yourself objectively if the title you began with still fits your novel as it has turned out.

If you haven't thought of a title up to this point, think about the kinds of titles you've seen on books in your target genre. Can you come up with something that's fresh yet "sounds" like a book in your target genre?

Select a title that has something to do with your story, not just a generic title. Your title should not only be fresh, but it should also be relatively short (this factor is also dictated by the genre) and easy for readers to remember.

Reread your manuscript for a phrase you may have used that would make a good title. Use the Title Brainstorming Worksheet on page 249 to list title ideas; then follow the instructions at the bottom of the sheet to decide which one you like the best. When you have decided on your novel's title, type it on your title page (see page 26 for title page guidelines).

Spit and Polish

You owe it to yourself to reread your manuscript now at least twice, looking for errors in grammar, spelling and punctuation, and for places where you can say something better. For best results, print out a hard copy of your manuscript, edit this copy and key your changes into your computer. Mistakes are just too easy to miss on the screen.

If you have a question about grammar or punctuation, refer to *The Chicago Manual of Style* (Chicago: The University of Chicago Press, 14th ed., 1993) or *Words Into Type*, Marjorie E. Skillin and Robert M. Gay (Englewood Cliff, NJ: Prentice-Hall, Inc., 3rd ed., 1986). For the final word on spelling, refer to *Merriam-Webster's Collegiate Dictionary* (Springfield, MA: Merriam-Webster, Inc., 10th ed., 1993). All three of these books make excellent additions to a novelist's library. (My book *The Marshall Plan for Novel Writing* contains The Novelist's Manual for Self-Editing, which you might find useful.)

Note: Do not run a grammar checker on your novel. These are intended for nonfiction and will not help you with your novel. Also, do not rely solely on your word processor's spell checker to find misspellings. It will not catch errors such as "He didn't no she was their."

Printing Out

When your novel represents your very best work, print it out in its final form. Use twenty-pound bond paper with 25 percent rag content. Place the pages loose in a manuscript or typing paper box. (For manuscript formatting guidelines, see page 25.)

To Market, to Market

If you haven't already researched agents and editors, do so now, giving this process your most careful attention. Then start querying and, if appropriate, submitting. The key is to start an aggressive marketing program. Your best effort deserves to be seen by publishing professionals. More than that, it deserves to be bought and read by people just like you—people who love nothing more than to lose themselves in a good novel.

"Genius," Thomas Edison said, "is 1 percent inspiration and 99 percent perspiration." The inspiration and perspiration are impotent without each other. You've used large portions of each to devise a genius that is uniquely yours.

May you know the pleasure and fulfillment of sharing your genius with the world, of seeing all your writing dreams come true.

Title Brainstorming Worksheet

Possible titles for my novel are:

_____   _____

_____   _____

_____   _____

_____   _____

_____   _____

_____   _____

My five favorites are:

1. _____

2. _____

3. _____

4. _____

5. _____

Choose between each of the titles one at a time by making a check
mark next to your choice on the list. Which title is your favorite?

1 or 2, 1 or 3, 1 or 4, 1 or 5

2 or 3, 2 or 4, 2 or 5

3 or 4, 3 or 5

4 or 5

The title that is check marked the most number of time is your
favorite!

Write it below, then type it on your title page.

_____

Index